USHERED OUT
OF DARKNESS

USHERED OUT OF DARKNESS

Finding Faith While Battling an Incurable Disease

by MICHAEL J. GARRIGAN

XULON PRESS

Xulon Press
2301 Lucien Way #415
Maitland, FL 32751
407.339.4217
www.xulonpress.com

© 2021 by Michael J. Garrigan
Edited by Kylie Yerka Herbert
Cover Design by Sara Jane Garrigan

Paperback ISBN-13: 978-1-6628-3063-1
eBook ISBN-13: 978-1-6628-3081-5

Dedication

To my wife Becky and daughters,
Colleen and Sara Jane.
In Memory of my mother and biggest
encourager, Marlene West.

Endorsement

I struggle with the thought of endorsing a book because I question my own credibility for such a task. What do I know anyways? As I thought about this, when it comes to books, I actually know a good deal. On top of reading the Bible cover to cover every year, I also try to read at least 50 other books annually to give me a well-rounded view of life and how to be a decent and productive human being. Mike's book, "Ushered Out of Darkness" is a work of love coming out of a lifetime of overcoming challenges. I agree with others that have encouraged Mike to write this because there are untold numbers of people out there that are hurting and that need the message of this book. Mike's ability to tell a story is fantastic. He weaves his life experiences into the unthinkable reality of knowing that he was going to be completely blind at some point. He uses humor, love and transparency that will make you glad you included this book onto your reading list, and ultimately into your personal library. I have a friend today that just found out that he too is going blind. I cannot wait to give him a copy of this book to help point him to tangible help and eternal hope for the next chapter of his life. Thank you for getting this book published Mike!

Matt Edwards
Executive Vice President–Mentoring Alliance

Foreword

T he gospel is Christ's redemption story for all of us. Embracing the power and understanding of the gospel will dramatically change your life. Jesus can turn tragedy into triumph. He can turn hopelessness into hope. He can turn darkness into light.

Over the years, Mike has become a friend of mine. We were once part of an intensive mentor group together. Jesus has dramatically transformed his life. Through a difficult childhood, a tragedy in his early years, and extreme obstacles, the gospel has given Mike a life worth imitating. His story is filled with challenges such as losing his father, being born with impaired hearing, and losing his eyesight, but Mike's hope in Jesus helps us to see the power of the gospel more clearly.

In *Ushered Out Of Darkness*, Mike's story demonstrates how allowing Jesus to give you a new perspective can completely change your life. Mike and his wife Becky are amazing examples of what it means to live lives worthy of the gospel (Philippians 1:27). A shining example of selflessness and unconditional love, Becky married Mike knowing the physical challenges that would eventually impact their life together. Mike overcame extreme odds to become very successful but then realized something was missing. A personal relationship with Jesus was the missing element in Mike's life. He surrendered his life to Christ as an adult and it changed him completely. Jesus gave him hope, a renewed sense of purpose, and a reason to live.

Mike's story is a perfect example of how God can use any situation or circumstance to radically transform one's life through the power of the gospel. Jesus and the gospel are the heroes of this story, but God has used Mike and Becky in mighty ways to encourage and give people hope.

This book is the story of Mike's life. I pray that it blesses you and encourages you to seek a full understanding of who Christ is and why it matters.

Michael Mullikin
NewSpring Church Lead Pastor of Operations

Table of Contents

Introduction xiii

Chapter 1   The Upbringing 1
Chapter 2   The Mentor 5
Chapter 3   The Distracted 9
Chapter 4   The Second Mentor. .12
Chapter 5   The Storm is Brewing 19
Chapter 6   The Named Storm 22
Chapter 7   The Jobs 30
Chapter 8   The Girl 38
Chapter 9   The Landfall 42
Chapter 10   The Two of Us. 49
Chapter 11   The Answer 52
Chapter 12   The Purpose. 58
Chapter 13   The Strange Dream .63
Chapter 14   The Third Mentor 65
Chapter 15   The Team 68
Chapter 16   The Sail Camp 71
Chapter 17   The Crewmembers. .75
Chapter 18   The Wheels 79
Chapter 19   The Giant Bumblebee. 82

Chapter 20   The Final Phase.........................86

Chapter 21   The Final Lap 90

Chapter 22   The Reunion 93

Chapter 23   The Search 96

Chapter 24   The Freedom...........................99

Chapter 25   The Perfect Plays 107

Chapter 26   The Dry Levee 110

Chapter 27   The Levee Refilled 117

Chapter 28   The Extraordinary 119

Chapter 29   The Lightning Rod 126

Chapter 30   The Leader........................... 130

Chapter 31   The Major Shift 136

Chapter 32   The Broken Streak 140

Chapter 33   The Dance 146

Chapter 34   The Queen........................... 156

Chapter 35   The Strong Finish.................... 159

Profession of Faith 163

Why I Decided to Write This Book................... 167

Tributes and Memories 171

Credits and Resources............................ 175

Introduction

Our family had a boat, a Boston Whaler I'd occasionally take out alone to a sacred place a few miles off the coast of Lake Erie. I would take this ride when I needed solitude or when something serious was on my mind and I needed time to think it out. I had never spoken a word about this spot to anyone. No one knew, not even my mother.

This sacred place was my prayer ground. Though I wasn't a regular Sunday morning church attender nor a Bible reader at the time, I did believe in God. I was a believer with no understanding of who God truly is. I had never heard of being born again and didn't understand the purpose behind Christ's death on the cross. I believed in God, but my belief was enveloped in arrogance. I expected to be served simply because I prayed.

I'll never forget what ended up being my last visit to my prayer ground. It was a hot, clear summer evening. As I looked out at the lake from the backyard, I could see the gentle waves lapping against the shoreline and hear the sounds of seagulls squealing. I let Ma know I was taking the boat out alone for a while. I walked out the back door, jumped into the boat, turned the key and ignited the engine. I pushed the throttle forward hard and sped out to the clear in a northwesterly direction. As I scanned the horizon, I spotted what must have been an 800-plus-foot Laker (a lake freighter, which is a bulk carrier of iron ore and coal in the Great Lake region). It was traveling a few miles out in the general direction I was heading, so I decided to check it out on the way to my spot.

When I finally reached the Laker, I carefully and respect-fully approached her and looked up toward the ship's stern. I could see a couple of crewmembers leaning against the rails having a smoke. Looking just below them, I marveled at the Laker's massive propeller plowing and churning the water like a giant hand mixer, pushing the massive hunk of floating steel through the waters with determined authority. While trailing behind the freighter, I decided to have a little fun. For the next several minutes, I was totally exhilarated and free as I zigzagged back and forth across the Laker's huge wakes, using them to surf and launch my Whaler airborne like a dol-phin. Satisfied, I waved goodbye to the crewmembers and left the area, heading further north for a half mile or so. When I reached the middle of the lake with nothing but water and sky in sight, I shut off the engine. I moved to the bow of the boat and lay down. I rested my head on a seat cushion and began to settle in as if I had pulled into a drive-in movie the-ater and was getting ready to watch a flick on the big screen.

I've always enjoyed watching the sunrises, sunsets and nature's spectacular storms roll across the lake, whether I was standing in the backyard of my mother's house or on the water, even sailing in storms. That evening, from where I was a few miles out on Lake Erie, I had a front row seat with an unobstructed view of the sunset. It felt like my own private world. There was an undisturbed peace in my prayer ground. It was absolutely silent and still, and I felt the presence of God. The work of the world's greatest author and painter was on full display as the evening sun began to set. Suspended in the palm of the lake's western horizon, the everlasting ball of fire reflected hundreds of thousands of glittering orbs across the lake's surface like giant dancing balls. The low-hanging, lazy sun dispersed a powerful ray of light into the western skies to create a perfectly draped layer of fine, red-wine sky. I slowly rolled my head toward the east, following the gradual changes of color to a deep, midnight blue across the eastern horizon. The panoramic view was stunning and surreal. What a finale. It was a delight to take in, and I swear for a brief moment the world came to a complete stop for a freeze-frame picture that branded an indelible image in my mind. I would hold that image for the rest of my life. Lake Erie was then, and is now, truly a special place to me.

Despite the awesome view, things were different that evening at my sacred place. I was filled with a combination of disbelief and anger, and yet there also was a numbness. I was having trouble comprehending the gravity of my recent diagnosis. The doctor had told me I had Usher Syndrome Type II. I didn't know much about this disease, but it appeared to be a massive, ugly storm approaching in the forecast of my life — a storm that would never rest and would last a lifetime. I had not experienced a storm like that before. The magnitude was something I wasn't so sure I could handle. I didn't pray this time while at my sacred place because I felt there was not much to pray for. I believed nothing could be done to change my situation. I simply stared at the horizon and wondered what the future would hold for me.

"I have vision today and, somehow, it will be taken away?" I thought. All I could think to ask God was, "Why?"

I interrupted my deep thoughts and made a decision. I pulled myself up from the bow of the boat and onto my feet. I was going to fight. It's simply not in my genes to give up and walk away.

Despite the dread and apprehension of the severe negative impact Usher Syndrome Type II would likely have on my future, I decided to continue on with my life and proceed with my plan to move to Atlanta, Georgia, after graduating from college. I was absolutely determined to weather the approaching storm of challenges this debilitating disease might rain down on me. I would fight through every obstacle, define the path of my life on my own terms and defy God every step of the way. I would handle this, and everything would be fine, I thought. I stepped behind the center console of my boat, started the engine and throttled toward home to pack my things.

Reflecting back, it's hard to imagine that day on Lake Erie took place more than 30 years ago. The memory is still fresh in my mind, heavy as an anchor, and causes me to shake my head in silence.

So what happened? I can tell you I certainly did what I was so determined and focused to do on that day. I fought. I fought hard for several years with every ounce of energy in what turned out to be the biggest battle of my life. I was swept out to sea hanging on to a capsized sailboat. The storm grew larger and larger as I aged, until it consumed me and then completely overwhelmed me. Eventually, Usher Syndrome Type II beat me down with a good ol' fashioned whooping to a resounding defeat. It left me in a state of near blindness. However, my defeat was not the end. That moment of defeat was the beginning of a remarkable journey — one from which I have come back with more determination and strength than ever before. The storm continues, but miraculously, I am still sailing through it, on course and undeterred.

Rather than what happened, the better question to ask is how this happened. The events of my journey have amazed me.

CHAPTER 1

The Upbringing

My childhood and upbringing could be considered idyllic. I lived most of my youth in a small Midwestern town called Vermilion, Ohio, located on the coast of Lake Erie. It was a destination for summer tourists who wished to enjoy the beauty of the lake, find refreshment in the cool breezes and escape the crowded cities. It was a place with a two-street downtown where locals and tourists alike could visit the soda fountain/pharmacy, bakery, hardware store, barbershop or movie theater. You could ride your bike around town, walk to the beach, visit the local maritime museum and walk to school. It was a place where kids could be kids, play outdoors for hours on end and run home when the street lights came on. Neighbors knew your name and looked out for one another. The sign marking the entrance to my hometown captured Vermilion's essence—Stay for a Day or Drop Anchor for a Lifetime.

I was born in the neighboring town of Wellington, Ohio, and whenever my mother recalled the story of my birth, she always told me I entered this world as a stargazer. This meant I was born face up rather than face down, which sounded fascinating, mysterious and special to me. I pictured myself staring up at stars in the dark. Little did we know darkness was something I would see again as I journeyed through life.

There were three children in my family, and I was the youngest. I had an older sister, Dolores, and brother, Paul, and we were all close in age. My mother had all of us by the time she was 25. My father was bright, determined, successful and very strict. He worked long hours as an air traffic controller, which left my mother at home spending endless hours raising three kids, keeping up the house and preparing meals for the family. She embraced it with enthusiasm.

My brother and I were 18 months apart and looked very similar. In fact, many people thought we were twins and constantly got us confused. However, Ma had a feeling our looks were not our only similarity. She noticed the way we were developing and reaching milestones was similar to each other, but different from the way my sister had developed. My brother and I were often unresponsive to sounds and didn't turn our heads when we were called. Ma tried to reassure herself the difference was because we were boys, but she had a nagging intuition in her core that made her look further for answers.

When I was 5, my parents sat in a doctor's office and absorbed the news that my brother and I had been born with severe hearing loss in both ears, which explained our unresponsiveness to sounds. It also provided an explanation for why we were slow to speak and had issues with pronunciation. The doctors had extremely low expectations for the two of us and told my parents we would never move beyond an elementary school education. They advised my parents it would be best to have us placed in an institution.

I had just completed a year of kindergarten that did not go well academically. Despite that, my parents declined the doctor's advice. They insisted on an alternative option of their own, equipping my brother and I each with a single hearing aid and enrolling us back in the public school system. Doctors had their doubts, but my parents stuck with their decision. I had to repeat kindergarten, but things went all right. It was not, however, without challenges along the way — and challenges to overcoming those challenges.

While in elementary school, I received speech therapy. At least once a week, I was taken to a quiet room where the speech pathologist silently moved her lips to read words to me. It was especially hard for me to distinguish the difference in the proper pronunciation of words with "sh" "ch" and "s" because I could not hear them. I sat and practiced a list of words with the speech pathologist, and I learned to understand what she read by watching the position of her lips, mouth and tongue. In my mind, I could silently hear what she had said. I quickly became a proficient lip reader. Eventually, the teacher could read entire paragraphs to me in complete silence and I could recite them back to her.

One of the biggest challenges in the classroom was when teachers turned their backs to write on the blackboard. Oftentimes, they would continue talking as they wrote. I lost the ability to lip read, and I had to depend on my poor hearing and one hearing aid. It caused me to miss a great deal of teaching, which turned out to be a frustrating and common problem in my schooling all the way through college.

You might wonder if any of the kids at school called me deaf and dumb or made fun of my speech, as young children tend to do to kids who are different. Sure, a few did. But they had forgotten about recess, that glorious time at the end of each school day when we went outside to the playground. That's where I routinely beat up the kids who made fun of me. Although it put a quick end to the taunting, I was regularly hauled off to the principal's office and faced my own consequences for fighting.

It was also during this time my father passed away unexpectedly. I was 7 years old, and my mother was a very young widow, left alone to raise three kids under the age of 10. But Ma was strong, brave and determined. She continued to raise us and encourage us to be the best we could be.

Chapter 2

The Mentor

Five years after Dad died, some guy named Richard West walked into our house. Ma had been secretly dating him for some time and made arrangements for him to come over to meet my brother, sister and me for the first time. He knew this meeting might be awkward and unexpected, so he decided to diffuse the situation with humor. When Ma introduced him, he walked in wearing a funny mask. It sure broke the ice and made for a great memory. Ma and Richard married in the summer of 1976 in the backyard of our home on the lake. And just like that, we three kids had a stepfather.

It took me time to adjust because I wasn't used to having a man around the house. I also was trying to figure out who this guy was and what he was all about. I came to the conclusion that my stepfather was a worker and he commanded respect.

The first change to take place around the house was no more eating dinners in front of the television. The TV was turned off when we ate at the dinner table as a family. Our step dad taught us how to set the dinner table and encouraged us to help bring out the food. During dinner, he would say things I didn't understand at the time like, "treat your neighbors like you would yourself," "slow to speak and slow to anger," "reap what you sow" and "always save money for a rainy day." When we were finished eating, we had to ask if we could be excused from the table. If we ate too fast, Dick would slow us down by not excusing us for a few minutes. If there were vegetables left on our plates, he would tell us to finish. When we were finally excused from the dinner table, he would remind us to push in our chairs. And then our chores began.

My stepfather didn't just command us, though. He led by example, teaching us kids how to clean the table, how to clean the dishes, put away food and wipe the table and kitchen counters clean. We were taught to sweep the kitchen and dining room floors. We learned to vacuum the stairs and living room often. At the time, I viewed these lessons as boring chores, but I later realized he was teaching us how he honored his wife and how we should honor my mother.

We had outdoor chores, too. Dick taught us how to check the lawn mower for oil and gas, check the spark plugs and sharpen the blade before cutting the grass. We learned how to rake leaves, shovel snow, change a tire and how to apply a coat of paint on everything he laid his eyes on. He showed us how to do something one time and expected us to do it his way, which was the right way.

As a teenage boy, work was the last thing on my mind. I wanted to hang out with my buddies and do foolish and crazy things. But in addition to chores at home, my stepfather had me working at the plumbing and HVAC shop he owned in town.

At the end of summer, I was promoted from my outside job titles of grass cutter, ditch digger and roof-tar worker to inside assistant. During those winter months at the shop, I was introduced to a broom, a dust pan, a bucket of hot water, a mop and a box of Spic & Span. Dick taught me how to do everything his way at the shop, just like he did with the chores at home. I quickly realized I was living with my boss wherever I was, and he had me working at every turn.

His motivating words would ring out: "Hubba! Hubba!" This meant hustle, as some might say, "get the lead out," and it echoed in my head day and night. He always seemed to be a step ahead of me and had the uncanny ability to catch my every shortcut. "Mmmichael John!" he would boom. I soon learned I couldn't do things haphazardly or take shortcuts to get the job done quickly. He took pride in the business he had built. He had invested a great deal of time and hard work, and I couldn't get away with anything.

Dick continued to teach me skills like how to cut and thread black steel pipe and galvanized pipe, run the cash register, install toilets, sinks and hot water heaters and even taught me how to clean out sewer pipes. My stepfather continued to mentor me for many years to come.

He was a conservative and humble man who generally was soft spoken, but he had a voice of commanding authority when needed. Through the years, I observed him in amazement while he somehow seemed to weather the difficult challenges in his life with ease. He just seemed so tough-minded, and I had no idea where he got it from. He was the smartest and hardest worker I had ever met. In fact, he was an engineer without a degree. He had an impeccable character and incredible honesty. His wisdom and integrity made quite an impact. I'm not talking just about me; he also had a lasting impact on his employees and some of my friends, too. I could sense their respect for him — and maybe a little intimidation — when he was near.

My stepfather also set a great example of financial responsibility for my siblings and me by not living "high on the hog," as he would phrase it. He talked to us about how to manage money, to spend it wisely and save for a rainy day and for the future. He introduced us to different ways of saving, whether through a bank account or investing in stocks, mutual funds or CDs.

Dick was a positive role model in every way possible around the house and also around his shop. But most importantly, I observed how well he treated and showed respect for my mother. What man would marry a woman with three teenage kids? The answer was clear to me: a man full of integrity, honesty, courage and character who truly loved Ma and wanted to be sure she was happy. I thank God for placing him in our lives. He was a heck of a mentor.

CHAPTER 3

The Distracted

As the years marched on from elementary to junior high school, our calendars and days were filled with everyday life and the activities of a typical small Midwestern town. During my junior high years, I tried my best to do well in the classroom and also was involved in track, football and basketball. My brother and I both are athletic, and we enjoyed playing on sporting teams and participating in neighborhood pick-up games. When I had free time from work, I enjoyed hanging out with my buddies. Fall and winter brought cool temperatures and lake-effect snow, Halloween, sledding, snow-fort building, snowball fights, cross country skiing and fun on the frozen lake. Summertime meant playing sports, riding bikes and activities on Lake Erie such as boating and water skiing.

There is one great summer memory that fills my mind when I think back on my junior high days. It was the summer sailing regatta race, and I remember it like it was yesterday. It was a partly sunny, wind day with perfect conditions for sailing. A loud "BOOM!" echoed across the lake from a cannon sitting on the bright orange starter boat. The two-day race was off and running. I had five friends as crewmates.

We took orders to prepare and perform tasks from the captain, the father of one of my buddies, who was positioned at the large sailboat's helm. He was a seasoned sailor who was highly organized and extremely patient with us. Most of the boys, including me, were inexperienced but extremely focused on the task at hand and eager to learn to sail. Only the captain's son knew his way around a sailboat.

We were just beginning to learn how to crew a sailing vessel on the job, so we were all excited when we were holding the lead within the first 10 minutes of the race. I thought it would be so cool if a bunch of kids pulled an upset and beat these old sailing veterans. But by the end of day one, we had slipped from the lead position to the middle of the pack.

Early the next morning, we were at it again. On race day two, my crewmates and I learned to take orders and raise the main sheet and the jib faster. We learned how to quickly prepare to tack and jibe when necessary. This was all very exciting stuff for me as a young boy.

We had just completed turning the corner of the final marker of the race and we raised the spinnaker to attack the finish line. While we made our approach, I kept my eyes on the surrounding sailboats. This was going to be a nail-biter finish. We were all tightly packed on the final stretch and had jockeyed toward the finish line. Two days of hard work had just come down to the wire. And we finished in ... last place.

In the end, winning really didn't matter to me. It was all about learning to sail and the adventures we experienced along the way. The race over, the five of us young boys relaxed at the bow of the sailboat, holding onto the rails as the bow submerged under the water. We dipped down into a large wave then shot up into the air above the water like an amusement park ride.

The bow submerged again and again, and we laughed our way back into port. I had the time of my life that day.

But not long after, some odd things began to occur. Occasionally, I would miss a pass on the basketball court or be surprised when I collided with another player who seemed to come out of nowhere. My family began to joke with me about being clumsy when I tripped on items left on the floor. At school, I sometimes bumped into people in the halls or ran into doorways. I told myself I was distracted, I was just getting adjusted to my growing body frame, those things happen to everyone once in a while. I wore glasses for nearsightedness, as did my brother. If, at times, my vision seemed to be less than perfect, I just thought it was normal for everyone's vision to diminish slightly with age, and I didn't give it another thought.

CHAPTER 4

The Second Mentor

As I entered high school, I was living life to the fullest. I was making great memories, enjoying school, having fun with my friends and all that goes along with the typical teenage high-school experience.

I made the varsity football team my freshman year, which meant hard work, lots of practice, taking punishing hits from upperclassmen and constantly proving myself. God also placed another mentor in my life during this time in the form of Head Coach Mentis.

A Korean War bronze-star medalist, Paul Mentis also was inducted into the Ohio High School Coaches Association Hall of Fame — one of the highest honors a high-school coach can receive. I had the privilege of being one his players.

It was Friday night under the lights when I saw Coach Mentis slam his clipboard to the ground. He was fuming and waving his arms on the sidelines. I had just missed a block, and the blitzing linebacker made his way into the backfield and easily tackled our ball carrier, forcing us to punt. I knew I had it coming for missing that block, so I purposely directed my approach toward the opposite end of the sideline from Coach. When I noticed he had moved that way, too, I redirected my approach back the other way and noticed he followed suit. He had locked his eyes on me and was waiting for me. There was no escaping.

Eventually, I arrived at the sideline, where I was grabbed by my face mask and greeted with a swift kick. I thought I needed a proctologist to pry Coach's foot out of my backside. He chewed me out good and made his point loud and clear. But he also offered encouragement. I wanted to tell him the linebacker came out of nowhere, but I kept my mouth shut, offered no excuses and just walked away when he was finished with me.

While taking a knee on the sideline, I absentmindedly pulled out my hearing aid and wiped the blood from my ear canal. (Plastic hearing-aid earmolds were the only type available at that time, and they were as hard as a gravel stone. When hit on the side of the helmet, the hearing aid had the propensity to gouge my ear canal.) I stared at the football field in frustration. It was my third year on the varsity squad and I continued to make silly mental errors. Other guys made errors, too; the game of football is never a perfect game. But I didn't think the other guys made errors as blatantly as I just had.

Yet this error felt different. It wasn't a mental one. I had a strange idea some vision problems on the field were what made me miss that block. It was like the blitzing linebacker was in my blind spot or something. It's hard to describe, and I couldn't quite put my finger on it.

As I mentioned earlier, it seemed these strange occurrences began in junior high — bumping into people and doorways — and they seemed to be more frequent in high school. It had become increasingly difficult for me to see at night, both on the football field and when driving a car. I didn't know what the heck was going on, but I never spoke a word of it to anyone other than my mother. I didn't want to sound like I was making excuses. I didn't know it at the time, but my vision had begun to deteriorate. I couldn't make sense of what was happening and, at that age, it never occurred to me I was losing my vision. The hearing loss was something I understood, something I had been born with, but why would I ever imagine something else might be wrong? Looking back, I'm glad I didn't know. The only thing I knew to do was try harder, be harder on myself and hope that Coach and my teammates didn't lose their confidence in me.

We soon regained possession of the ball, and I was thankful when Coach put me back on the field. I had to improvise, so I developed a habit of locating the linebacker in each play prior to the snap of the ball. I didn't take my eyes off of him until I knew I placed him firmly on his back or I cleared him out of the way for our ball carrier to run for daylight. The fear of what Coach would do with his other foot if I should mess up again was all the motivation I needed, and I never missed another block ever again for the rest of the season — and the next one.

Like my stepfather, Coach Mentis was a man who taught us to do things his way, the right way, and do it extremely well — and always better than the other team. He also taught us winning doesn't come free, and it sure doesn't come easy.

"Winning requires a lot of hard work," Coach would say. He was right about that. He had a God-given gift to deliver incredible pre-game speeches that would rival Knute Rockne's famous "Win one for the Gipper" speech at the University of Notre Dame. It was inspiring, and our team responded well. Coach Mentis instilled in us that it wasn't about what we couldn't do but about what we could do as a team. We were respectful of our coaches and our equipment managers, including one who was challenged. This particular guy showed up to work rain or shine. He performed his equipment manager duties admirably, and he never complained about it. He earned respect and was treated as a member of our team.

We also were respectful of our opponent, and trash talking was not part of our game. We were unselfish and close knit. We loved and respected one another like brothers. Each person on the team I stood with had earned the love and respect of his teammates. We earned it when we completed the infamous grind of Coach Mentis's summer conditioning workouts, known as the "12 and 12."

The workouts consisted of a 400 meter track and steep stadium stairs. Monday through Friday for six weeks in the heat of summer, we lined up on the track and waited for the whistle that signaled the beginning of our sprint around the track. Without a break in momentum, we moved to the stadium stairs where the whistle started us off on a swift-paced climb up and down 10 times. That was considered one set.

We repeated this — once around the track and 10 times up and down the stairs — until we achieved our initial goal of six sets.

Each week, the bar was raised, and after six weeks we were completing 12 sets in a day.

But we couldn't stop there! We learned that 12 and 12 was just a name, not a limit, as Coach Mentis and the coaching staff challenged us to achieve 14 sets. There were no breaks between sprints or between sets. We had just enough time to throw our hands above our heads to draw in a deep breath of oxygen. But for some guys, these were a few seconds to puke, wipe their mouths, swallow the bitter stomach acid, then ready themselves to sprint again when the whistle blew.

And all this doesn't include everything Coach put us through before the start of each grind. We'd be gasping for air before the 12 and 12 even began. It was difficult to make it to the finish each day, and those six weeks seemed to go on forever.

Coach Mentis wasn't just training our bodies. He trained our minds, too. We had a business-like team demeanor and were taught to control our emotions. We were never to let the excitement level get too high when we found ourselves ahead of our opponent, nor were we allowed to drop too low when we found ourselves behind. We were an even-keeled team, no matter the score, and remained focused through all four quarters.

I recall a highly anticipated mid-season conference game where all this training came into play. We were one of two undefeated teams. It was a Friday night. It was an away game for us, and the stadium was packed. Every seat was filled with a fan, and more were standing around the perimeter of the fence surrounding the field. We kicked off, and before we knew it, our opponent had punched us in the mouth and shut us down. We were clearly beaten on both sides of the ball in the first half and went into the locker room at half-time trailing by a score of 19-7. Coach didn't chew us out; he merely settled us down. We knew what we needed to do. We maintained our poise, and we returned to the field for the second half with a quiet focus.

We methodically and consistently blew our opponent off the line of scrimmage and attacked them with our suffocating defense and our down-hill offensive ground game. It was a thing of beauty.

By mid-third quarter, the opponent's defense was lined up and precisely pointing where they anticipated we would run the ball. We knowingly telegraphed the play to them as our offense lined up practically in the same formation and ran the same predictable three or four plays straight up the middle between the tackles repeatedly for the entire second half. Over and over, we challenged our opponent to stop us. They couldn't, and we won the game 19-27.

There was no doubt the game was a difficult grind against a very good football team. There was no doubt it was a classic one-for-the-ages ball game with a lot of talent on the field that night. Yet there was no doubt Coach Mentis's infamous 12 and 12 summer conditioning workouts were far more difficult and had prepared us for this game.

Coach's demands had given us mental and physical leverage over our competitor. We simply wore our opponent down. But even more, we were propelled to victory by the valuable lesson that nothing comes easy and to achieve goals and finish strong, you must put in the effort and preparation. Finishing strong is not an inherent talent or natural ability embedded in our genes at birth. It requires willingness and commitment to work tirelessly and put ourselves in the position to know how to finish strong.

We were a very coachable group of young men with high expectations and a hunger to win, and boy did we win with Coach Mentis at the helm. How sweet it was to win back-to-back-to-back conference championships for three seasons. I can still see Coach Mentis with a celebratory cigar hanging from his mouth and hear him saying, "Winning sure is fun!"

He was right about that, too.

CHAPTER 5

The Storm is Brewing

When I wasn't playing football or working for my stepfather, I often could be found on Lake Erie either waterskiing behind our family boat or sailing.

There is an old maritime saying: Red skies at night, sailors' delight. Red skies in morning, sailors take warning. It was on the morning of one such red sky that my buddy and I dared trespass on the foreboding waters of this great lake and test the limits of our sailing skills. Lake Erie had come alive with anger and unleashed her power with fury, emptying her arsenal of Nor'easter, turbine-force winds that produced huge, relentless, rolling white-capped waves. She commanded respect, and she clearly sent signals that all were unwelcome in her waters that day.

My buddy and I respected Lake Erie but couldn't help defying her warnings that day. He set out on a small, 14-foot Laser sailboat, sleek with its lightweight fiberglass hull built to ride low and close to the water level. I moved my Boston Whaler just outside the mouth of the Vermilion River, which leads out to Lake Erie, and tucked my boat just behind the much-needed protection of the break-wall. Besides us, there was not a single boat in sight.

The skies were dark with low, rolling clouds and rain falling horizontally. I stood in my boat waiting for my buddy to return. He momentarily disappeared between huge waves before popping back into view like a cork. There he was, riding a wave on his Laser sailboat, completely exposed to the elements outside the break-wall, with no protection at all. Of all my friends, he was the best sailor around. We embraced the challenge this weather brought and took turns sailing the Laser. We switched boats every 45 minutes or so as one sailed back in to seek the shelter of the break-wall and to catch his breath.

It was my turn to take a beating from the harsh weather. Adrenaline pumping, I dove into the water and climbed aboard the sailboat. I quickly buckled my life vest, pulled the mainsheet in and snapped the mainline in the cleat. I got a firm grip on the tiller handle extension, and it was secure in the palm of my hand. Then I threw my feet under the foot-strap. With the weight of my body hiked out to the side, I looked up toward the mast and saw the mainsheet ripping and snapping violently in the high winds before it netted a puff of strong Nor'easter wind. Within a nanosecond, the freakish ride began. I was shot out like a cannonball into the wide open of the great inland seas. There was no amount of imagination that ever came close to matching the actual thrill and the immense challenge of being tossed around like a small piece of driftwood on those waves.

Our continued defiance seemed to further agitate the lake. She flexed her muscles and made many attempts to reach out and grab us with huge waves. She tried to sweep us off her turf with the forceful winds, but we were young, fearless and determined.

Then I was unexpectedly bulldozed by a rogue wave that slammed the sailboat on its side. I was washed off the boat. I worked to climb back onboard by standing on the center-board of the capsized sailboat, trying to right her in the midst of the high winds and seas. My buddy and I loved the phys-ical challenge and thrill and just kept going back out for more.

That was a ridiculous ride in one heck of a storm. Thankfully, we lived to tell the story.

Little did I know this powerful storm would one day pale in comparison to some of life's storms I would face in my future. I could not have imagined the biggest storm of my life was brewing and bearing down fast.

CHAPTER 6

The Named Storm

After high-school graduation, I packed my bags to prepare for the next chapter of my life. I entered college at Ohio University, about four hours from home in the foothills of the Appalachian Mountains in the southeastern Ohio city of Athens. The campus boasted stately brick buildings with white columns and walkways paved in brick woven among pristine green lawns and hardwood trees. It was beautiful and extremely collegiate. I enjoyed college life and easily adjusted. I met a great new group of friends, and we attended extracurricular events and parties or just hung out.

Ohio University has two huge annual events — Halloween and Springfest. These were awesome days filled with good times with my new friends. I only wish I could remember more about them!

My transition to college life eased even more when I learned Ohio University had a competitive water-ski team that competed regionally with other college ski teams in three major events — slalom, trick and jump.

I tried out for the team and made the cut. It felt good to be back in the water having fun. I competed in the trick and jump events. Our team enjoyed our travels to college campuses around the region for competition meets and the complete college experience. Not only did we have fun, we also won regionals and met the qualifications to compete at the National Collegiate Waterski Competition in Louisiana. We were thrilled for this opportunity and even more thrilled when we wound up placing fifth in the nation overall.

Everything seemed to be going well during my early college years. Especially when I received a second hearing aid while at home during a break.

From the time I was 6 years old through college age, my audiologist had recommended only one hearing aid. I never knew what I was missing until another audiologist asked me if I had ever thought of wearing two hearing aids. I tried it, and I was suddenly keenly aware I had missed a tremendous amount of information through so many critical learning years. The unbelievable difference in having two hearing aids hit me when I experienced something new on my walk home. I heard birds chirping like I had never heard them before. It was like I had been listening to everything on an old transistor radio and suddenly everything was in high-quality surround sound.

I was not at all concerned with what people thought of my hearing aids. They were what they were, hearing aids behind both ears. They were and are a part of me, and they are an extension of my everyday life (kind of like how today's younger generation feels about their cell phones). I also wore glasses for my nearsightedness, and I saw the hearing aids as just another instrument to aid me. I didn't care if people noticed them. In fact, while in college, I decorated them. One hearing aid was covered in red glitter star stickers while the other sported a "Lite" sticker, as in Miller Lite beer. The decorations were a hit.

Life was good, and there was no significant sign of any troubles ahead until I decided to check into contact lenses. While at home during a summer break from college, I left work at my stepfather's shop and headed to a scheduled appointment with the local eye doctor. He seemed to spend an exorbitant amount of time on the examination, and he remained quiet while he shined a bright light directly into my left eye, then my right eye and back to the left eye again. I remember thinking, "Is this really necessary for contact lenses?" The doctor left the examination room for a few minutes, then returned and resumed his examination of my eyes for a little while longer. He finally spoke: "I think you may have what's called Retinitis Pigmentosa, RP for short."

"What?"

I was shocked and unclear on what this meant to me. The doctor referred me to a well-respected ophthalmologist in the area and strongly suggested I be seen right away.

"But what about the contact lenses?" I remember thinking naively.

That was the first bit of knowledge that something bad was happening with my sight. The storm's outer band had made landfall, but she was still quite far from unleashing her havoc.

I was in my early 20s when I sat in the ophthalmologist's examination chair, going through what seemed like an endless battery of tests and having bright lights pointed directly into my fully dilated eyes.

Finally, the exam ended and the ophthalmologist confirmed the initial diagnosis given by my local eye doctor. He believed I had a rare, inherited retinal degenerative eye disease called Retinitis Pigmentosa. However, that wasn't all. The Retinitis Pigmentosa coupled with my severe hearing loss was described as its own disease and classified as a syndrome called Usher Syndrome Type II.

"What?"

More disease terminology I had never heard of in my life. My mind was racing while I was trying to comprehend.

The doctor continued speaking in great detail and described the syndrome's impact. "With this disease, your retina will deteriorate and you will eventually lose your vision to blindness. The beginning stages of retina deterioration will start with night blindness, then you will lose your peripheral vision, then the macula of your retina will deteriorate as you age, eventually leading to blindness. This will result in a series of challenges, from simply walking across a room to crossing a street to walking in the halls," he said.

My head was spinning, and still he spoke: "You will eventually have to stop driving. Everyday tasks will eventually become more challenging and you will have difficulties living a normal life." And before I could ask the obvious question, he said, "There is no medical cure to prevent the retinal deterioration."

He also confirmed the disease affecting the deterioration of my retinas had already begun its march. However, there were no definitive answers for how much vision I would lose or if the deterioration would ever stop. My mom and stepfather were in the examination room with me, and I heard my mom trying not to cry. I sat in the exam chair stunned and speechless. I lowered my head, leaned forward toward my knees and exhaled around the kick in the gut that had just been delivered.

The technical definition for Usher Syndrome Type II is a rare genetic disorder caused by a mutation in any one of at least 11 genes resulting in a combination of hearing loss and visual impairment. It is a major cause of deaf blindness and is at present incurable.

Usher Syndrome Type II is characterized by hearing loss and gradual visual impairment. The hearing loss is caused by a defective inner ear, whereas the vision loss results from Retinitis Pigmentosa (RP), a degeneration of the retinal cells. Usually, the rod cells of the retina are affected first, leading to early night blindness (nyctalopia) and the gradual loss of peripheral vision. In other cases, early degeneration of the cone cells in the macula occurs, leading to a loss of central acuity. In some cases, the foveal vision is spared, leading to "doughnut vision," where central and peripheral vision are intact, but an annulus exists around the central region in which vision is impaired.

My non-technical definition of what Usher Syndrome Type II means is as follows: I was hit with a very rare, double-whammy that involves severe hearing and vision loss. I was born with severe hearing loss that was not discovered until I was a young child. My vision would deteriorate in a slow drip in the coming years like some cruel joke.

After a week of thinking about my diagnosis, my shock shifted to rage and anger. I went out with my buddies and got absolutely inebriated. I purposely drank excessively. I just wanted to wash away this disease. I wanted it out of my body and out of my mind. My reality, my dreams and everything in my future seemed to be over. All of it. While a buddy drove me home that night, all the disappointment and despair came pouring out. I cried like a baby ... and I puked plenty.

There is no cure to prevent the deterioration of my retinas, no way to stop this disease. Just like that, everything changed. I was left wondering what kind of quality of life I would be losing and what quality of life I'd be left to live. The thought of not being able to perform the simplest tasks like crossing streets was incomprehensible. If I have trouble with that, how am I going to get a job? If I can't drive, how am I going to hold a job? Future wife? Who the heck would want to marry a guy with this debilitating disease? Having a family seemed to be out of the question.

I couldn't understand how something like this could just drop in and interject itself as a permanent fixture in my life. All I had done was walk into the local eye doctor's office for contact lenses. I walked out with a disease I had no understanding of at all.

Life was going so well after overcoming so much already. I never expected I would be forced to face more serious challenges. I was left wondering, "What's next, for God's sake?"

Although graduating with a degree in communications with an emphasis in photojournalism and a minor in business management was probably not a good career match for someone who was recently told he was going blind, I am not sure what would have been a match. But I had dreams of working for National Geographic or Sports Illustrated as a photographer and traveling the world. Throughout my studies, I had taken some innovative pictures I still have today, but my diagnosis stopped me from pursuing this career path. I'll never know for sure, but those dreams probably weren't likely to happen. It was too late to change my major, but photojournalism did encourage me to think outside the box and come up with ideas that would prove critical later in life.

The ophthalmologist's confirmation that I had Usher Syndrome Type II provided an explanation of why my hearing had been robbed. Already in the process of experiencing night blindness, I had an answer for why I had missed that block playing football on that Friday night.

I understood this disease had begun its attack, and it was well prepared to wreak havoc for the remainder of my life. I was at a huge disadvantage. I felt so ill-equipped for dealing with something I had no idea how to prepare for. Lack of preparedness typically leads to failure.

Any assurance I'd had for my life had been squashed. I was afraid of what was coming at me, yet I decided to move forward with an uncertain future anyway. I graduated college and, when the summer came to a close, I prepared the Boston Whaler for the winter. It would be the last time I would go through that ritual for many years. In my car were a few bags packed with clothes and a full tank of gas for the long trip to Atlanta, Georgia.

CHAPTER 7

The Jobs

I t was a fall day. I drove 12 hours south and arrived in Atlanta in the late afternoon. It was 1987, and the recession made finding work difficult, but I found a job bussing tables to pay for utilities, food and gas. I was searching for a full-time professional job and, eventually, I was hired to work for a computer technology firm in an entry-level position.

Looking back, I can see God orchestrated my introduction to the owner of a computer technology contracting firm willing to take a chance on a recent college graduate with no experience. However, I couldn't see it then. In fact, I had no desire to work with computers. I didn't have a computer degree, nor did I possess much computer knowledge. Besides, I thought computers were dry and boring. Only geeks worked with computers. My hesitations were proven wrong when I gave the world of technology a chance. Once I started working in the field, I began to really enjoy computer systems. The technical field soon became my passion and ultimately became my professional career for the next 30-plus years. I became a geek, and I loved it.

I gleaned technical skills and ascended the learning curve by attending training courses and reading technical books late into the night. There seemed to be no end to the new things I could learn. I also picked up a second job as a computer operator, working the night shift for the next few years in addition to my full-time job. I figured if I immersed myself in learning it would eventually pay off.

I put my experience and knowledge to work and applied for higher-level technical positions, which proved to be challenging during the economic downturn. I was employed by a contracting firm working with a major, worldwide computer technology company that went through a major restructuring. Many loyal employees who worked their entire careers with this firm were soon laid off or offered early retirement packages. Like many of the company's contractors, we soon found ourselves with a cancelled contract. We were all left looking for new jobs. It wasn't the only time a position I held ended abruptly, but I gained valuable experience, and I continued to move ahead and seek out new opportunities.

Interviewing for new jobs is never easy, and I remember one that especially frustrated me. I had been selected for a first interview and my qualifications were a perfect fit. I was called back for the second and final interview with high expectations of a job offer. The second interview went absolutely swimmingly until they noticed my hearing aids. I thought nothing of it at first. Then I began fielding a number of questions on the severity of my hearing loss. We finished the interview, and I never heard from them again. I was discouraged. My hearing was not a factor in my ability to perform the job functions needed. My hearing aids worked well and did exactly what they were meant to do — aided my ability to hear. But for the interviewers, my skills were overshadowed by their perception of my hearing aids. Disheartening as that was, I moved on. They'll never know they passed up a hard-working, dedicated employee. However, their decision to not hire me would prove to be another critical step in getting me closer to that awesome job waiting somewhere out there.

Although I was getting my foot in the door for interviews, I needed to find a way to stand out from the competition. I leafed through technical journals and magazines looking for networking groups and postings that would help me learn more and meet other technology professionals. I came across a listing for a technical user group that included a phone number for potential new members. I made a call to find out how to join, hoping to broaden my contacts.

A gentleman answered and indicated he had no idea about the posting or the user group. He checked with his secretary and confirmed they had not created a posting or authorized any listing in the magazine. I checked the phone number to verify I had dialed correctly. He confirmed that I did. I thought it was strange. I offered a quick apology and was about to hang up the phone when the man interjected and asked if I had a resume I could send him. Of course I said yes.

It turned out this man was a recruiter (we called them headhunters back then), and was able to line me up for an interview with a company he worked with that had an opening. Things went very well, and I was offered a job with their information technology department a few days later.

Within 18 months, the company decided to decommission the existing computer systems and business application, and we deployed the latest, leading-edge hardware and software. The enhanced responsibilities, technical skills and expertise I would gain from this position would prove to be just what I had been searching for to differentiate me from the competition in the future. I just hoped a hiring manager, somewhere out there, would look beyond my hearing aids and hire me for the skills and capabilities I possessed rather than passing me over for what they perceived I couldn't do.

Strange how things work out. That's what I thought at the time. I considered myself lucky to get this job, and gave it no more thought. Today, I think differently. When I look back on this opportunity and the surrounding circumstances, I can see again how God certainly was in control and made a way for me that was not mere coincidence.

I worked at this company for five years, from the late 1980s through the early '90s. What an amazing job this turned out to be, and I had a great manager. On a personal level, he also was a great mentor who looked after me. For example, after each annual pay raise earned, he escorted me to the human resources office and said, "Mike just received a raise. He now wants to increase his contribution to his retirement plan." It meant a lot to me that he chose to give me the opportunity to learn the latest and greatest technical applications. It meant even more that he shared with me some lessons from his life experience, including saving for the future.

Our company also had great management and a CEO who was co-inventor of fiber optics and was inducted into the National Inventors Hall of Fame. We were the industry leader in providing raw quartz, which was used for many applications, including in the world-changing high-speed fiber optics used for telecommunications.

We had a small IT department and built our own leading-edge data center from the ground up. I was determined to learn and succeed in the opportunity I had been given. There were many occasions when I worked late into the night and didn't leave the office. I slept under my desk or in my car in the parking lot, waking up every hour to check on the progress of a business application upgrade or the resolution of a critical technical issue.

We eventually installed the company's first commercial secured router and hub devices that made remote-access connectivity possible. The world was changing. More and more companies were implementing remote-access solutions. Although we had the capability, company policy required all employees to be in the office during normal business hours. We were permitted, however, to work remotely after hours and on weekends. I didn't mind. I could see this new technical path had the potential to allow me to continue working should I become unable to drive someday in the future.

Around this time, I had gone home to Ohio for a few days to visit my mom and step dad and was returning to Atlanta by plane. I sat at the airport talking with my stepfather while waiting for my flight. I needed his advice. I told him my technical skills and experience were now in high demand and thought it might be time to strive for higher-level technical positions. He offered words of wisdom he drew from his own experience. The day he started his own HVAC business, "I thought I knew everything, then realized I didn't," he said. He encouraged me to continue to prepare, continue studying and to learn from mistakes and failures with every step forward. "Nothing comes easy," he said.

Shortly after our conversation, I landed a dream job with an iconic worldwide technical company with a world-class reputation. I didn't know, of course, but I would work there for the majority of my career — my final 18 years as an IT professional. Within my first year with the firm, the CEO made a huge change that went in my favor. The company implemented a cost-cutting initiative to consolidate many offices across the country. Those employees affected were given a choice to work from another office location or work remotely from their homes. It was an easy decision for me. For the next 17 years I would work remotely from my home office, and I would not have to worry about commuting as my eyesight continued to diminish. Again, I thought it was strange how things worked out. But, again, God had a hand in arranging this for me and my family, too.

"Put in the work and pay your dues," my step-father would say, and that I certainly did. I never viewed myself as deserving a job simply because I was drawing breath. I viewed it as something that must be earned. Putting in hard work and paying your dues is the key to earning that next promotion.

I took this lesson to heart and worked extremely hard to earn my job every day. I consistently sacrificed things like time off and sleep to meet the demands of my clients and reach the goals my company set. If I didn't, I knew someone else would, and I was determined to succeed. Forty-hour work weeks became a rare exception. When they did occur, it felt like a part-time job. Most weeks consisted of 60 hours or more, and I took my responsibilities for my clients and my team very seriously. I cared deeply about my performance and the performance of my team, as well as our ability to meet or exceed our client's goals and deadlines so their businesses didn't sustain adverse impacts.

Another motivation in my work was the fact glaring in the forefront of my mind: I had no idea how much time I had left to perform my job. I didn't know if the slow-drip deterioration of my eyesight might suddenly escalate, resulting in blindness. This fact propelled me to strive for perfection. I gave the utmost attention and focus to every project as if it could be my last. In that respect, it made me a very driven worker. I was looking to perform at my best while the opportunity to do so was still there.

My technical path during my journey with vision loss gradually moved me away from tasks that required entering technical commands via keyboard strokes and toward a leadership role, eliminating the risk of entering incorrect commands as my vision grew worse. The foundation of leadership I had been taught by my early mentors served me well as the technical team lead. I was well-prepared for the focus and hard work required to do the necessary research, to gather information and allow it to unfold so I could lead my team to make sound decisions.

The cool thing about working remotely was nobody — my teams, my managers, my customers — had any idea about my poor hearing and vision. We all worked in different parts of the globe, and I used an excellent speaker phone on my desk with excellent volume controls. It was equipped with Bluetooth technology that could be paired with my Bluetooth hearing aids, which allowed me to hear fairly well and did not give any indications of my poor hearing for quite some time.

It wasn't until I traveled that my team members from around the globe realized I was not only hard of hearing but also visually impaired. But they never allowed those disabilities to change their perception of my ability to be their leader, and I appreciated that. Everything was going well.

CHAPTER 8

The Girl

I was a few years out of college, living on my own in Atlanta, and I was learning my way into adulthood. As I was gaining new technical skills at my job, I also was figuring out personal finances, health and retirement benefits, financial investing and how to navigate large purchases like a house and a vehicle. I had a lot of questions, and I knew the right person to ask — my stepfather.

When discussing things with Dick, he never made decisions for me. He would offer sound advice and left the decision-making to me. I called often to seek his thoughts. He always took the time to listen, and he provided valuable guidance.

At the end of one of these discussions, he threw a very pointed question at me, and, although it was right on target, it also was embarrassing.

"When are you going to marry that girl?" he asked me.

"That girl" was sitting next to me and overheard his question.

She was beautiful. I met her in Atlanta at a party held at my apartment complex. There were lots of people and fun activities. I remember there were door prizes given to the holder of the transparent plastic cup that bore the number matching the one called. During the course of the party, I went to the bar and asked for a refill. I handed the bartender my cup, and noticed he returned it to the wrong person, someone on the other side of the bar. I considered my cup lost and started to ask for a new one.

But something nagged me about that cup. I was confident I had the number that would win the top door prize of the night, so I chased after it. When I finally fought my way through the crowd and reached the other side of the bar, I found my cup in the hands of this girl with beautiful brown eyes. I walked up to her and mentioned she was mistakenly given my lucky cup. We laughed and introduced ourselves. Her name was Becky, and we talked with instant ease about all sorts of things for the rest of the night. My number was never called, but my lucky cup certainly won the top door prize. I asked Becky out and took her to an Atlanta Hawks basketball game on our first date. We immediately fell in love, and I learned she had much more than beautiful brown eyes. She had a heart of gold and impeccable character.

We went on a lot of fun dates — whitewater rafting, amusement park rides, dinner on a train ride through Atlanta and boating. We even attended a Billy Graham Crusade in Atlanta because my stepfather suggested it, but I felt a bit uncomfortable. I kept wondering why all these people had their hands raised in the air.

Although we were having a great time together, something began to bother me. I still had not mentioned a word about my disease, and Becky had no idea I might lose my vision someday. She knew, of course, I had severe hearing loss. My two hearing aids had given that away. It didn't seem to bother her, but how would she react if I told her about the serious impacts that come along with Usher Syndrome? This disease would not only impact me. It would have a parallel impact on her if we stayed together long-term. She might decide not to sign up for this and break off our relationship. I knew the future I could provide her was uncertain. I knew it wasn't right of me to keep this information from her for much longer. I knew I had to get this conversation over with soon.

Every week, I felt the pressure to tell her grow, but I couldn't find the right words or the courage. In hindsight, maybe I should have told her way upfront, when we met. It would have been a lot less painful, but we were having such fun, and I didn't want it to end. Depending on how she responded, our relationship could end immediately. When I did finally tell her, I knew I'd be able to see her response simply by looking in her eyes.

One Saturday night, I gathered enough courage. Miraculously, she had heard of this rare disease in her high school biology class. She actually knew what Usher Syndrome was. "It doesn't matter," she said. "I love you." I thought that response was just a bit too quick. "Are you crazy?" I couldn't help but ask. "Did you hear what I said? I may lose my sight, and it will have a severe impact on you, too, if we continue our relationship and get married someday. Do you understand?"

"Doesn't matter," she replied. "I still love you." "Do you want time to think this over?"

"No."

Her eyes said she meant it, and she did not allow my debilitating disease to prevent her from saying "Yes!" when I proposed to her after dinner at our favorite Italian restaurant on Valentine's Day in 1993.

On an April evening one year later, we were married outside a historic antebellum home in downtown Roswell, Georgia. The setting and the weather were perfect for our special day. We danced at the reception and celebrated with family and close friends. We were excited and looked forward to our future together.

I could not have fathomed just how difficult things would get as we ventured through life together. It was one thing to talk about the eventual impact of my disease, to know it intellectually, but it was another thing altogether to live it out. The speed of the approaching storm was a huge contrast to the perfect weather on our wedding day, and it took me by surprise. Within eight years of our marriage, I had already experienced significant vision loss. This disease waits for no one.

CHAPTER 9

The Landfall

I was 30 years old when we married in 1994, and I was honored to have my stepfather serve as my best man. My wife and I purchased a starter home in Cumming, a rural area north of Atlanta. Four years later, we moved to Alpharetta, Georgia, a suburb north of Atlanta where we would live for the next 20 years. We both had good careers, and we expanded our family with a couple of dogs and two beautiful daughters. We had it made. We were living what many would consider the American Dream. There wasn't a single visible scratch or blemish anywhere on the outside.

On the inside, however, I was drowning in misery beyond my wildest dreams. The cruel deterioration of my peripheral vision was at full throttle. It was an excruciating transition from the seeing world to the world of blindness. I had no idea, from one day to the next, what I wouldn't be able to see anymore. The never-ending uncertainty was torture. My peripheral vision didn't narrow in an exact circle like you would normally think of tunnel vision. Rather, pieces and parts within it were suddenly gone. These changes didn't happen at the same pace or in the same manner in both eyes, either. My right eye deteriorated faster than the left, as if wanting to be the leader in some crazy competition. I tried to adjust to each new visual field, but the changes were so constant the "new normal" never lasted long. There seemed to be a different new normal every day.

I hit rock bottom, and I was dragged across that rocky bottom for several years — both emotionally and physically as my increasingly poor vision often led to collisions with doors, walls and curbs. I sustained gashes on my shins and a bloodied forehead as I ran into, tripped over or failed to duck objects I couldn't see. My despair built with each stumble, fall and crash. My frustration, anger, resentment and bitterness rose to off-the-chart levels, followed by humiliation, embarrassment, shame and feelings of failure. In my attempts to avoid the vicious emotional cycle, I leaned toward the protection of isolation. With it came depression, and I fell deeper and deeper into total anguish.

Usher Syndrome was not satisfied with robbing me of my hearing at birth. My negative emotions were like protein powder, the core ingredient in a potent recipe that fueled the disease's progression. It quickly gained unimaginable strength and developed into a Category 4 hurricane.

The eye of the storm made landfall in my life with thunderous authority and savage clouds that blocked out the sun like heavy drapes pulled tight across a window. I wasn't ready.

Since discovering what Usher Syndrome Type II really was, I knew a storm was coming, but there was no place to hide, no way to outrun her. Like a scheming villainess, it snuck up. No one knew her next move. What was in store?

When would it happen? It seemed just a short time ago this disease had lain dormant inside me. It was cocooned in my genes, using my body as an incubator and building strength for years before waking to steal my vision.

I had been preparing for this moment, but when the eye of the storm and I finally met up close, she was more horrible than I had imagined. She was, and is, a disgusting monster like the harpies of mythology — a long-clawed snatcher, vicious and cruel. I've never seen such ugliness in my life. I would soon learn this disease wanted much more than my hearing and vision.

I was in the throes of an epic war. I'd been bluffing for years that I could kick this storm's ass in my own strength. I believed I could maintain the upper hand and control the situation through sheer determination.

The disease called my bluff. Her strong winds unmercifully battered me. I was flattened by their force. I had tried to protect myself and my family through isolation and by wearing anger like armor, but she swiftly neutralized all my efforts.

She had wrapped me in her powerful wings and I was trapped before I knew it had happened. The storm and I were locked in a battle being waged inside my body, vying for the most prized possession: my soul. There could only be one winner. How could I keep control of my will, my mind and my body? Something had to give.

The disease seemed to have its own mind. The harpy knew with confidence and arrogance time was on her side. She wasn't going anywhere. She would be lurking inside me, planning her next move, for the rest of my life. She thought she was unstoppable. My own strength was nothing to hers. She would never relinquish her grip; I would always feel her claws grasping. She could stir up the waters and winds and inflict damage and suffering on her whim. She could take whatever she wanted, whenever she wanted it. She didn't need my permission; she had no restrictions. As long as my strength was neutralized, she could have her way. I would be left hanging on to that capsized sailboat, incapable of righting it on my own. There appeared to be no escape. This storm would destroy my life; I would drown in its raging waters.

Then an interesting and attractive change caught the eye of the storm. Becky was now holding on to the boat with me. She was determined to keep our marriage together and keep our heads above the waves. The harpy was pleased, and I gulped in a lungful of water as her plan became crystal clear. She was upping her game, shooting for a hat-trick.

If I should succumb to the raging waters, the storm knew my wife would follow, and then the entire family. This was the ultimate goal. The knowledge made me especially ashamed I had brought Becky into this awful mess with me. I could not let the storm win. But the barometric pressure had dropped to 935 millibars and the storm beared down hard, charging forward with intensified might. The waters swirled, and white-capped waves and relentless headwinds caused agonizing pain as they attempted to separate me from Becky and the boat. There was no sign of this storm slowing. Instead, somehow, she continued to strengthen.

Every day for years, I demanded and pleaded for this disease to stop its progression, but she stared me down with a confident smirk and raised her middle finger. Then her smirk became a look of determination. She tightened her grip on the handlebars, pumped the gas for the tease and ruthlessly accelerated the onslaught of destruction. I was hurtling ever closer to a world of complete darkness.

My demands were useless, and the situation was hopeless. I did not want to be a blind man, but there was then, and is now, no cure or medical procedure to stop or prevent this disease.

As the deterioration escalated, I never had a desire to hide my pain and sorrow in a haze of drugs and alcohol. I faced the storm's wrath head-on and completely sober. But when I felt too weary to tread water and keep my grip on the capsized sailboat, my only other option began to dawn. I could simply let go and be rewarded with instant relief.

Although I never took any serious actions, I must admit thoughts of taking my life were dancing in my head during the most difficult moments. I couldn't win either way. It felt like the storm would claim victory whether I held on or let go. "Checkmate," I heard her say as she watched my every move, saw the moment my panic set in, laughed as I began to struggle like a child swept too far out from the shore by the riptide. I was exactly where she wanted me — emotionally isolated from those who loved me. It seemed it was just a matter of time before my fingers slipped and I was sucked under the waves.

I was a kid when the huge Laker the Edmund Fitzgerald mysteriously sank. It was no mystery to me now how the sailors must have felt "when the gales of November came slashin'," as Gordon Lightfoot sang about the wreck. I was going to sink, just like the infamous freighter.

I managed to tighten my grip and batten down the hatches, but as the storm continued to rage, I continued to battle on multiple fronts with stress, anxiety and fear. At work, I had a negative attitude and was quick to complain. But maintaining my job was crucial to maintaining a roof over my family and paying the bills. I felt the weight of this every moment of every day. Fear and shame made me their captive as I became more and more incapable. I was deeply embarrassed when my family could see my suffering. I felt I had let down my wife, daughters, mother and stepfather.

All the while, the storm was reaching new magnitudes of disruption and destruction. She was consuming me, and I was thoroughly overwhelmed. Carrying the weight of my struggles was like hauling up a heavy anchor with an endless chain, and I didn't know how much longer I could keep pulling. This storm had taken its toll on my body and mind and continued to chip away at my grip. I was totally exhausted. I knew I was near my breaking point. Any hint of hope was blown away on gale-force winds as soon as it appeared. My thoughts and emotions were a storm of their own, spinning around like a twister and annihilating any joy that surfaced in my life.

Incredibly, even at these lowest points, I still had the audacity and determination to grind this out on my own.

I was living in complete defiance of the storm's promise to overtake me. I denied all help from my wife and pushed her further away. Despite everything, I had this pretentious notion I was still in control. And God? He wasn't even an afterthought. I was convinced there was nothing he could possibly do to save me from my conviction. I was sentenced to lifelong incarceration in this stinking hole of darkness.

CHAPTER 10

The Two of Us

While the storm raging inside me was terrifying, I always loved being outdoors to experience the power and beauty of crazy weather. I had paid close attention to the weather reports all week. Category 4 Hurricane Frances made landfall in Florida and continued her path inland toward Atlanta, Georgia, where she became Tropical Storm Frances. When I heard she was headed my way, I was determined to prepare my 14-foot Laser sailboat to meet her.

I took my boat to Lake Lanier, a large lake north of Atlanta. As I stood on the shore, Frances's presence astonished me. I could hear the roar of the wind as it ripped through the trees and swept across the lake. It sounded like I was standing right next to a railroad track while a freight train rumbled past.

By all accounts, the storm was downright intimidating. That I was eager to sail in her winds brought my sanity into question. Still, the storm's demonstration of nature's wind power was too attractive to resist.

As I studied the storm, a reality struck me. I knew in my gut with the current rate of my declining vision, my driving days were coming to a close, which would bring my sailing days to a close, as well. With that thought, my sanity check was over; I made up my mind to seize this opportunity to sail.

I launched my Laser and readied myself with feet securely strapped and the weight of my body hiked over the starboard side. The mainsheet quickly lassoed a powerful gust of wind and I was slingshotted into the open water. Riding the storm was a riveting rush of adrenaline. It was as though Frances lifted the hull and threw me across the surface of the lake like a skipping stone. The speed with which I sliced through the water had the centerboard generating a vibrating, humming scream. I fought to hold steady while the slightest movement of the tiller caused my sailboat to react suddenly and drastically. I let out a crazy laugh while I battled the high winds with every ounce of effort I could muster. It was a never-ending workout as I enjoyed this insane but thrilling ride.

There were just two of us on the lake that day — me and God. I cried out to him in frustration and anger as I faced the reality of my disease. I yelled like a lunatic, challenging the tropical storm to bring all it had to offer. I was like Lieutenant Dan in a scene from "Forrest Gump."

"I'm drowning and I have no answer," I said, in case God didn't already know. I certainly did not expect God to give me answers.

At day's end, I was completely exhausted. It was exhilarating and satisfying to think I had successfully battled Frances. Yet, I had a sickness in the pit of my stomach. I felt helpless, lost and vulnerable. I had battled the storm raging outside, but I was standing at the edge of defeat in the battle with my disease raging inside of me. I packed up my Laser and headed for home.

Little did I know at the time, but God had heard my unorthodox prayers, and the answer — just like the path of that tropical storm — was heading my way. Like the familiar refrain of a Bob Dylan song, "The answer, my friend, is blowin' in the wind. The answer is blowin' in the wind." I just couldn't see it yet.

CHAPTER 11

The Answer

My wife was well on her walk with Christ at this point in her life, and she attended church regularly with our daughters. I, on the other hand, attended church only on a few occasions, and always with a lack of interest as I listened to what was being taught in the sermon.

My attendance was transactional. I was checking a box, believing if I showed up a few times I would head to heaven someday. I had never opened a Bible, nor did I watch sermons on television. I had never been receptive to people who tried to talk to me about Christianity, or any religion, for that matter. I was skeptical when I saw people get all giddy or joyful about church and God, like it was some awesome club to which they belonged. I thought it was nuts and not for me. I didn't understand it, so I ignored it and kept things to myself.

Sitting in the sanctuary with my family, the lights dimmed, I often would rest my chin in the cup of my hand and try to keep my eyes open. It was hard to fight off the sleepiness that inevitably overtook me during the sermons. Then, one morning, I was caught off-guard. The pastor was about to launch into his prepared message, and I was ready to settle into my routine, which typically led to my Sunday morning nap. But before I could assume my normal pose, the pastor interrupted himself and went off script. What he said would forever change the course of my life.

God was compelling him, he said, to say something specific to someone somewhere in the sanctuary. His next words were spoken deliberately and intently.

"You were never meant to carry the weight of your struggles and sufferings. You were never meant to carry the weight of your stress, your frustration or your fears. You were never designed to do so. Let God handle it. He's the only one who can."

There was total silence in the sanctuary while the pastor stared toward where my family and I were sitting. Then he walked to the podium and began his planned sermon.

I was stunned. My brain was shouting: "Get outta here with that nonsense! You've got to be kidding me! This has to be a staged act!" I silently protested and my blood pressure rose. I had never spoken a word to that pastor in my life. I had never spoken a word to anyone, and especially not in this church, of my deep internal battles.

But I couldn't get over the pastor's words. "There's no way!" my brain continued to accuse.

How could I have been singled out in this sanctuary full of people on the very day I just happened to show up? That message could have been for anyone, but why was I listening? Why should I believe those words? After all, they are just words, aren't they? But at the same time, something was different about this. Deep down in my gut, I knew I was the sole target of that off-script message. It was meant for my ears to hear on that day.

They were words I never thought I needed to hear. I didn't ask for them. I never sought God nor prayed to him for help because I didn't believe he could help. Though I stared directly at the pastor for the whole 30 to 40 minutes of his sermon, I had no idea what he preached about.

That wasn't the message I was intended to hear. I was there to listen to that off-script message, those few sentences that spoke volumes directly to me. They were resonating in my mind, replaying in my ears. I wanted to hear more and understand their meaning. I had never felt so positively captivated. I just kept thinking how bizarre this whole experience was. (I would learn later the "bizarre experience" was actually the work of the Holy Spirit.)

Those off-script words were a message from God with instructions. Yet I still couldn't fully believe their authenticity. "Was it truly for me?" I kept thinking. This had never happened to me before, and I had no clue what I was supposed to do with it. There was no bullet-point project plan listing orderly steps to follow.

Keep in mind I was a stubborn guy set on proving I could control things in my life even though I knew I couldn't. I was not a Bible scholar and could not have made any of this up. The following paragraphs are my best attempt to describe what took place as I started taking tiny steps of curiosity that became steps toward understanding.

Typically, after hearing what the pastor said, I would have brushed it off and dug deeper in the trenches like a stubborn tick, continuing to rely on myself to fight a losing battle. But instead, I felt led to do something unthinkable in my estimation. I gave up the fight. I had been doing the same thing over and over for years, hoping for some pivotal turning point to occur in my life — some kind of positive outcome — but it hadn't happened. I was tired, and I was at my breaking point. I couldn't continue down this path. It had sapped both my strength and my energy, and I couldn't sustain the fight any longer.

Exhausted, I knelt and looked up toward the storm. I raised my hands in surrender and nodded my concession. I had just had enough. It was over. I was done. I let go of my grip on self-reliance and I tapped out of the wrestling match.

I stunned myself with this decision to call it quits. As I rose to my feet, I lowered my head in shame for what I had just done, and I began to walk away.

It was here — in this moment of defeat — where the turn in my remarkable journey began. As the storm moved in for the kill, I heard an unexpected, familiar sound from my high school football days.

"Railroad!" "Railroad!"

It was an audible we used to signal for a change of play at the line of scrimmage. Our coaches didn't teach us that; we just made it up. We used the audible as a decoy and to have some fun, but we only used it a few times. The funny thing about it was we never actually changed the play. (No one dared change Coach Mentis's play.) However, the audible gave the opposing defense the impression we had switched the play, which was the whole point. It kept the defense guessing.

"Railroad!" "Railroad!"

The storm sent out her defensive line like an evil villain's henchmen, but it all went down so fast, they never had time to react. This was no football game but a play in the game of life, and mine was at stake.

It was a quick bang-bang play, executed with absolute precision.

The moment I surrendered, the storm's arrogant confidence turned to confusion. Her man shot the gap, then realized he had fallen for the decoy. My big right tackle met him with a powerful, sweeping force, pancaking him to the ground in an unexpected, vicious trap block.

This left a gaping hole in the line, and I took the handoff. It was smooth and swift with a glove-like fit. I was not carrying a football; I was carrying my soul. I tightly secured it with both arms and planted my foot to cut upfield. I lowered my shoulder and busted through an approaching linebacker like a bat out of hell.

"Whoa Nellie!" I imagined college football broadcaster Keith Jackson jumping to his feet in the booth and shouting that famous line. "This guy has come alive and is showing a determined fight for his soul!"

I drove a deliberate stiff-arm in the face of the next would-be tackler and gained momentum as I turned the corner to outrun the second level of defenders.

Fullbacks do not often get called to run the ball. God called my number and I had to make the most of it when decision time arrived. It's a decision many put off for later, as I had been doing. But later suddenly became today and today suddenly became now. The call to decide had come, and it was — without a doubt — the single most important and most impactful decision in my life and for my life. Once it was made, I quickly pressed forward with it and ran for daylight.

I sped down the straightaway near the seams of the sideline, heading for the end zone.

The end zone in this game held the freedom that came with accepting those instructions in God's special message for me, and I never looked back.

CHAPTER 12

The Purpose

"The two most important days in your life are the
day you are born and the day you find out why."
– Mark Twain.

God is to handle all my baggage, not me.
I accepted the simplicity of that instruction I heard in
the off-script message, and I agreed to try to understand it.
That's all I did, not realizing it was all I needed to do. I was a
bit apprehensive during these early stages of following God.
I was expecting disappointment, and I was prepared to beat
a quick retreat if something I learned did not hold water.
There were no contracts, nor was I forced in any way to stay
and participate. I could check out at any time.

It didn't take long for me to start questioning God's
promises. If he truly is the only one who can handle the enormous weight of my sufferings and bondage, why do I let my
challenges control my attitude? Is it possible to separate the
daily struggles and circumstances from my ability to experience joy? I searched and found the answer was yes. It was still

difficult for me to comprehend how this could be, but I was learning God's words are true and trustworthy.

I discovered the centerboard of my boat was Christ, and when I found my footing on him, he began to teach me how to right my capsized sailboat. I was still figuring out how to keep the keel of my soul centered on Christ through this intimidating storm. It was daunting to look up at the huge, white-capped waves that surrounded me like a mountain range of challenges. But no longer would I take on this storm alone. It was going to be a long haul. It was going to take time and patience and a lot of investment in God's word. But it would be worth any risk because I would learn to sail through this Category 4 hurricane. Though the waters would be rough, I would not capsize.

Having answers left no excuses not to take another significant step forward in my spiritual journey. I decided to be saved by repenting of my sins and completely surrendering my life to Christ. When I accepted God's gift of grace, the power of faith in Christ began to set in. I experienced exhilarating freedom from the bondage I'd felt for so long. It was like the adrenaline rush of a 100 mph free fall when you jump out of a perfectly good airplane at 15,000 feet. The transformative process of being ushered out of darkness had begun.

For the first time in years, I felt relief. I stopped thinking about myself, my struggles and my sufferings from the disease. I stopped seeing through the familiar viewfinder of the world — how unfair life was, how easy it was to whine and hold on to self-pity, resentment and bitterness toward others. I changed my focus to God. It was sobering and humbling when I realized it was me, not God, who needed to change. In my resistance to see the world through God's viewfinder, I had cheapened who he really was. I believed he had no power to help me, yet I hypocritically pointed blame at God for the bad things that happened to me and the world around me. It was so easy to pray for things I desired and gripe when I didn't get things exactly my way. Sound familiar?

These realizations helped me accept that life was not meant to be fair on my terms. My life was meant to be in God's hands. I was ready to be part of God's plan and solution for the troubles of this world. I was finally able to experience true sustainable hope that would not be blown away by the storm. God equipped me with a new attitude. I was still determined, but there also was humility. I began to live a very purposeful life with full trust and faith in Christ. He provided an unobstructed path away from all fears, failures and shame. I became a very driven person in my work and with everything in my life, especially things that affected my family. I felt strangely bold, relaxed and unafraid. I received the gift of salvation.

Once I had experienced the authentic freedom of living in Christ, of living outside that hole of darkness and breaking free from the slavery of blindness, I wanted more. So I stayed engaged and continued to learn who God really was and how to recognize and be grateful for the gifts he gives.

I've accepted I will go blind. I don't have to like it, and I certainly don't. But that's not the point. It's that while I go blind, I have a choice to make. I can let this storm take control and drive my life to misery. Or I can look for, accept and be thankful for the gifts and fruits of the spirit God has given and continues to give. Christ suffered and sacrificed greatly when he gave his life on the cross so he could give me life everlasting. So while walking the walk with him is difficult and I know I, too, will suffer, I will suffer in his great name, giving thanks with each step even as my eyes fail me.

Never did I ever expect this transformation. Never did I dream the words I heard in that off-script message would provide my pathway forward through the storm. How quickly it all began to unfold seemed way too simple against the complex struggles I battled every day.

That this truly was my pathway became even clearer during a weekly men's Bible study group. There, I had a stunning revelation about my stepfather. My mind wandered back to when I was a teenager eating with my family at the dinner table. I thought my stepfather was speaking in some strange tongue when he would spout seemingly random words of wisdom. It now hit me he had been quoting Bible verses. My stepfather, always a thinker and always a planner, had intentionally planted seeds for our ears to hear, even though I didn't pay any attention to it then (or so I thought). Stumbling upon this knowledge, I understood how my stepfather weathered the storms in his own life. He carried a look of assurance, confidence, determination and certainty throughout each day, and he had an incredible, unwavering resolve no matter the circumstances. I suddenly recognized those traits as his faith in God, and I was simply amazed.

Even though my stepfather had passed away a few years before I made this discovery, his words continued to impact me. I knew with confidence the road I had chosen to travel was the road he traveled, too. I knew, without question, I was headed in the right direction.

CHAPTER 13

The Strange Dream

I had a strange dream and couldn't make sense of it, but it stands out in my mind to this very day.

The dream took place back in my hometown of Vermilion, Ohio. I was walking across the Liberty Avenue Bridge, which crossed over the Vermilion River, which flowed out to Lake Erie. It was a clear, sunny day. There were no cars, no boats, no pedestrians. There was complete silence everywhere while I walked across the bridge. I looked up and saw a childhood buddy of mine riding toward me on a bicycle. He stopped in front of me and asked, "Where are you going?"

"I'm not sure," I said.

I looked over the rails of the bridge toward the river below and wondered where all the boats were. I turned back around, and my buddy had ridden away.

That was it. It made no sense. It held no significance — until I received a phone call from that buddy shortly thereafter.

The two of us make it a point to talk at least once a quarter during the year to catch up on things like family, Vermilion High football and Ohio State Buckeyes football. He called me one day, but this call struck me as odd. We had just talked about a month earlier, so there wasn't much more to add that we had not already talked about. And his tone of voice was different; I could tell there was something important he needed to talk to me about.

After a few minutes of general conversation, he finally got to the point of his call. He began to speak about what was weighing heavy on his mind. It was a topic we had never spoken of before, and it was the most serious conversation we'd ever had in our long friendship. It was a risk. He had no idea how I was going to react. I might accept it, or I might tell him to shove it. Yet it meant enough to him that he was willing to put our friendship on the line to have this conversation with me.

I listened without interruption as he explained his hope and prayers for me to find my path toward Christ and be saved. I've known my buddy since the second grade, and this was the boldest thing he had ever said to me. There was total silence for a few seconds after he finished speaking. I was deeply moved and had a smile on my face. I cleared my throat and told my friend his prayers had recently been answered. This wasn't the type of thing we guys ever talked about. We just never did. Perhaps we should have earlier. Taking this kind of risk is what it means to be bold in Christ like the disciples who risked their lives to deliver the Good News.

CHAPTER 14

The Third Mentor

I t wasn't always easy for me to take that risk of being bold in declaring the Good News or to behave in a godly way. The day I joined Kevin's conference call for the first time comes to mind. I thought I had entered a lion's den. Most of the people on his call worked in another country, but a few worked from different parts of the United States. I quickly noticed Kevin was somehow very capable, even via phone, of grabbing someone by their shirt collar and pulling them nose to nose with him as he demanded results while giving some encouragement.

I was the new guy on this team serving a very large customer account, and the honeymoon was over within a week or two of joining. My first phone meeting with Kevin seemed like a martial arts championship fight in the middle of a caged canvas mat. We did not see eye to eye on things. With our tempers flaring and blood pressures soaring, we aired our differences with gloves off. We swung our fists to bloody each other's noses and attempted the knockout blow with a knee. It seemed apparent we would not work well together. It was a very unpleasant call. I'd never experienced one like that before, nor have I ever experienced one like it since.

It took time to recover from that call but, without realizing it, our fight was the turning point for us. We never apologized to each other, but we quietly agreed to move on from it, and a month later, I rejoined Kevin's scheduled conference call along with the other team members.

This time, something told me to keep my mouth shut. As I listened with my phone on mute, I began to hear Kevin from a different viewpoint. Maybe I had initially misunderstood him or jumped to conclusions. I have no idea if he thought the same about me, but it didn't matter anymore. After a few weeks sitting quietly on his conference calls, I concluded we had a lot more in common than I thought and were on the same page about most things concerning work. I came to a new understanding of who Kevin was as a leader and his expectations for us to lead and produce results.

Over time, the two of us talked plenty during the day and night to help each other meet our global responsibilities. We talked about technical issues that needed resolving and plans for projects to push our enterprise-level customer forward through the fast-paced evolution of technology (cheaper, better, faster, smaller). Kevin later became my boss and my mentor on this account, and we worked together as effectively as pistons in an engine. He had the utmost confidence in my ability to lead. He trusted my instincts, my wisdom and my judgement to make tough decisions, which meant the world to me. I did the same for him, and gave him my utmost respect and appreciation.

Kevin was incredibly smart and had tremendous passion and perseverance. He wasn't afraid to use his booming voice to command attention. He certainly wasn't afraid to set tough, extremely high standards for all to follow, including me.

I would like to think we had become close friends, but I think it was more of a respectful business relationship. We held each other accountable on work-related issues, but never on the personal or spiritual fronts. However, Kevin did become a guy with whom I could share funny experiences related to my vision, like one that took place while traveling on business in Malaysia.

With limited vision, travel can be quite the challenge — even in my own country with familiar places. This time, I was in a different country with a completely unfamiliar setting. I was in the hotel lobby and asked an employee to tell me how to find the restroom. I thought I had followed the directions and pushed open the door. I nearly jumped out of my skin as I met a woman in a burqa whose eyes were large as saucers as she let out a scream. Of all the wrong places I could be, I was standing inside the women's restroom! Blindness has its humor.

Kevin and I served together five years, then moved on to other endeavors. We never spoke again. I regret not sharing my faith with him and wonder if we would have become more than work friends if I had. With the way things had begun between us, I certainly would never have guessed I would gain another awesome mentor in Kevin. I thank God we crossed paths.

CHAPTER 15

The Team

When I learned how to walk with Christ completely, it changed who I was at work. I began to enjoy my job with absolute passion. It didn't feel like work anymore. Although I had been a hard worker and dedicated employee, I was quick to complain and voice my dissatisfaction with others. I was transformed into a quiet doer, and it led to earning the global technical leadership position I mentioned earlier. I was humbled and grateful.

I felt it my mission to perform and serve at the highest level worldwide and to use the blessings of my job — my compensation — to support the work of the church. I contributed for mission trips, to help those in need of food and shelter and to spread the gospel of true hope and salvation.

I'll always be grateful I was given the opportunity to lead some of the best technical minds the world had to offer. Each member of my large team stationed around the globe did their part to top-gun levels. Along with their skills, they each were the right fit for the right job for the right team. I call it the "locker room fit" because every member was a very strong team player.

They worked extremely hard and extremely well under immense pressure and time constraints, and they did it with passion. We developed a strong family bond and a deep level of trust. No matter the time of day or night, everyone pitched in to ensure the client's work got done. This special group of people performed at a worldwide elite level, and they earned all of the credit they received for their achievements. Time after time, our team successfully completed major, complex technical projects. It felt a lot like winning and it sure was fun! However, what made this a well-respected technical team at my company and what made it special to me was that the members remained humble and carried themselves with integrity, honesty and character.

Although I was never in a position to preach the gospel to my team while at work, I leaned on the Bible to provide me with the necessary guidance and core values required to be their leader — to have a servant's heart, to lead with character and integrity, to think of others more highly than yourself. These are things that business schools and Management 101 courses do not offer, but are extremely valuable. Jesus Christ's leadership model is often the opposite of the way of the world and the traditional views of business.

I'm awfully humbled to have been along for the ride and to have been part of this phenomenal group I called my second family. When I composed my final email to the team before retirement, I was able to share a Bible verse that meant a great deal to me, Joshua 1:9, and I hope it impacted them as well: "Have I not commanded you? Be strong and courageous. Do not be afraid; do not be discouraged, for the Lord your God will be with you wherever you go."

CHAPTER 16

The Sail Camp

"How in the world have you been able to get around the house like you do?" my wife asked on our way home from the ophthalmologist. This was the first significant sign we were not on the same page when it came to understanding how much my vision had declined and how little I could actually see.

"Anybody can get around the house blindfolded, can't they?" I responded. At home, where everything was familiar, the depth of my vision loss was not apparent because I learned my surroundings. Since my job allowed me to work remotely from home, and I did so for long hours, I did not often go to new or unfamiliar places, so Becky hadn't realized how much of my sight I had lost. She was stunned when I couldn't locate the ophthalmologist's finger until it was directly in front of my eye.

I had created this gap of understanding over the years by rejecting all help from Becky and pretending I was still in control of the situation. I knew my suffering brought immense concerns to my wife, who has an "I need to fix it" personality, but she could only step aside and watch me as the disease marched on. Perhaps I was trying to protect her when I pushed her out of the way, or perhaps I was just being prideful. Either way, the result was we didn't talk about my suffering for several years. When I accepted the off-script message and began to learn who God was, we were able to start closing that gap. When I learned to stand on the centerboard of Christ, I learned to do so with Becky by my side. Together we discovered how to right the capsized sailboat as if we were being taught at a sail camp. The sail camp was God's word, which provided stability for both of us to learn to ride through the storms together. Along the way, we began to talk more, and I slowly began to let her into my world.

My wife was instrumental in supporting me during my walk toward blindness and my walk toward Christ. We talked often about a message or a verse delivered at a Sunday morning church service or at a small group Bible study. She had a way of explaining things so I could better understand. This simple act strengthened our marriage.

One of the biggest challenges we faced together throughout the course of this disease was the sudden negative impacts of my vision loss. Though it was gradual, in the world of Usher Syndrome Type II, it is impossible to forecast anything. This made it a struggle for both us to prepare and plan for changes whenever they might occur. We knew the storm had come, but we had no clue what tomorrow's weather would bring. We didn't know when or if I would be completely blind, we didn't know what the impact of blindness would be on our lives ... and my wife is not at all comfortable with changes without detailed information on what to anticipate.

We learned to do something very difficult together. I had to build my trust in Christ while letting go of responsibilities I could no longer handle. She had to build her trust in Christ to take on the additional responsibilities from me. One of those big responsibilities was driving. My wife became the only driver for our entire family for many years, and she drove us everywhere. My kids and I jokingly called her our bus driver. She gained other major responsibilities later in our marriage, as well. After years of working part time with preschool-aged children, Becky had to re-enter the workforce full time and eventually became the sole income provider for our family.

During the difficult times, my wife maintained an unwavering willingness to step out of her comfort zone and step up to the plate, putting her trust in Christ to carry the additional tasks.

I married a very special lady. Not only did Becky not allow my debilitating disease to prevent her from saying yes when I proposed, she also did not allow it to prevent her from standing by my side through years of challenges. She was committed to sticking to her promise to stay with me for better or for worse. After more than 25 years of marriage, she's still with me. Like I said earlier, I undoubtedly won the top door prize the night we met.

Besides our wedding anniversary, there is another annual symbolic reminder of how far we've come together in our marriage. Every Christmas, my wife and I unbox an old, 2-foot plastic Christmas tree held by a plastic basket, and we place it in the dining room. It was our first Christmas tree.

It was all we could afford during our first year of marriage. That tree is a reminder of how simple things were back then, and it has come a long way. After all these years, that tree is still standing and looks pretty good. Likewise, our marriage has come a long way, and it's still standing and looks pretty good, too.

Moving forward together, there is something appealing and comforting in knowing as we grow in Christ together and grow old together we also grow more in our love for each other.

CHAPTER 17

The Crewmembers

I am honored God gave me the opportunity to cut the umbilical cord at the deliveries of both of my daughters. I held their precious little bodies in my arms for the first time and heard their little cries that let the world know they had arrived on earth. What a miracle! A lump developed in my throat and I got goosebumps all over. Those baby girls stole their daddy's heart from that first moment and kept it forever after. They instantly became my most precious gifts from God.

I was determined to be a father involved in my daughters' lives and tried to turn every moment into a lifelong memory. I'm ecstatic to have developed calluses on my knees from giving galloping horsey rides through the living room. We performed countless cheerleading skits and danced away many childhood nights. I also was quick to take advantage of the once-in-a-lifetime opportunities to teach my daughters how to swim and ride bikes. What a thrill to experience joy through their smiles, their laughter and the excitement in their voices. I enjoyed fatherhood more than I could ever imagine.

Our daughters were always surprising me. They learned at a young age how to outwit my wife and me. They asked their mother if we could go out for dinner. Mother said no. Unhappy with that answer, they quietly walked upstairs and found me in my home office, which was at the opposite end of our house. Not only did they leave out the part that they already asked their mother, they also rephrased the question:

"Daddy, do you want to go out to dinner with us?" "Sure. Let's go."

Their eyes lit up as if they'd just won a game of bingo. They raced down the hall, down the stairs, past their Mother in the kitchen and into the garage. They hopped in the car and sat buckled in their seats with smirks on their faces. I passed my wife and said, "I'm ready. Let's go."

That's when we learned we had been played by a couple of little kids.

That night my wife pulled into a parking space at a restaurant and we all stepped out of the car. I waited for my wife to come around to the passenger side to help me cross the parking lot. I was struck speechless when my daughters grabbed their daddy's hands instead. They took the lead and told me when the coast was clear of cars, then they assisted me safely across the parking lot. This was something they had quietly observed their mother do many times. My knees went weak as I was overwhelmed with joy.

As my daughters continued to grow, my vision continued to degrade. At age 40, by definition, I was legally blind. I had completely lost more than 90 percent of my peripheral vision in both eyes and had developed what is sometimes called tunnel vision or doughnut.

I was determined not to lose hope while I continued to lose the visual ability to see my kids grow. My presence was all that seemed to matter to them, so we continued to find ways to create memories together. We spent countless hours swimming at the pool, boating and waterskiing as a family.

When my kids hit their teen years, they started driving. With only their learner's permits, they often asked me to ride along. It soon became obvious to me my girls always seemed to ask me rather than their mother because they figured out I would remain calm and say little about their driving as I blindly sat in the passenger seat like a potted plant!

With their teen years also came new anxieties, whether it be a sporting activity or a school exam. So my wife and I taught the girls the importance of putting in their best effort, proper preparation and prayer. Then I would follow it up with, "Do your best and let God do the rest." We hope they will carry those words with them, as a reminder of who is in control, for the rest of their lives.

There's another message I also hope they'll carry with them forever — the one of how much I love them. I was never taught sign language, but a friend taught me how to sign "I love you." Since they were little girls, I've used this sign to communicate with my kids whenever we were at a distance. Whether they stood on the starting blocks at a swim meet, on a lacrosse field or at high school graduation looking for me in the stands, I flashed my "I love you" sign so they could locate me. "They see you and are smiling and waving," my wife would say. It was my way of showing them I love them and I'm here for them — even if I can't physically see them.

My kids, now that they are grown, always honk their car horns before driving away from our home. It's how they acknowledge my "I love you" sign as I stand at the other end of the driveway. They are now driving off to return to college or to their own place in Atlanta. It amazes me how raising my daughters brought awesome responsibility, and I am struck with awesome gratitude for the amazing young ladies they have become.

CHAPTER 18

The Wheels

Even though I was now legally blind, my car still sat in our driveway. I wasn't driving it anymore, but it was like some symbolic reminder that I was still trying to hang on to my independence. I used to drive that car with my dog hanging her head out the back window barking at passersby as we headed around the corner to Starbucks for a cup of morning coffee. I drove my kids to daycare sometimes, and in their early elementary school days I let them sit on my lap and steer the car from our house to the end of our street. Lots of good memories were wrapped up in that car.

When my daughters got their licenses, I asked each of them if they wanted to drive it. "No. No thanks," they quickly replied. I wasn't ready to give up, but even the prospect of having their very own vehicle wouldn't sway them. When I told them I would give it to them, they both said they would never be caught driving that car in public.

In fairness to them, it was a 20-plus-year-old Honda Civic, but I was still a proud owner. I treated it more like a pickup truck than a car over the years I drove it. There was something gratifying about pulling my workhorse out of the home improvement store parking lot hauling a load that would typically require the capacity of a Ford F150. I'd have lumber sticking out the windows, the backseat and trunk filled with piles of bricks and bags of dirt and lawn care equipment in the passenger seat.

To cool off my sweat-soaked back in this four-door beauty, I cranked down the windows and took full advantage of the old-fashioned air conditioning — mother nature's wind hitting my face. I smiled and laid my left arm out the driver's window and the other on the steering wheel, just like I remember my grandpa used to do. I seem to remember he even had a similar car back in his day. The dashboard of my car was a simple, no-nonsense dash, equipped with only a speedometer and a gas gauge. No fancy gadgets, no bells and whistles.

Then one day, I woke up feeling fully content with getting rid of my beloved car. It was a Monday morning. I picked up the phone and dialed the number to No Longer Bound and asked if they would come get my car. I thought I'd be upset to let it go, but instead the decision felt right. I was still hanging on to my car because it made me believe I was still in control. But I realized my tunnel vision would make it impossible to drive it ever again, and I was being selfish, stubborn and unreasonable. I was done with those adjectives. They would only get me or someone else hurt. Holding on wasn't worth the cost, and the realization brought me absolute peace in donating my car.

Just like that my driving days were over, but my decision to let go would change lives.

No Longer Bound is a Christian organization that provides drug addicts refuge and treatment. My donated car would become a tool to teach the skills required to repair and restore a vehicle. Once restored, that old car would answer the prayers of a family in need of reliable transportation. What better way to make a positive impact on people's lives than by giving something I can no longer use to someone who desperately needs it?

Not long after I let go of the car, I realized my road bike was another one of those things I was holding onto.

I was first inspired to take up cycling after my brother rode his bike across the United States with a buddy one summer while in college. His three sons followed in their father's footsteps a few years ago by cycling across the country, this time with the purpose of raising money for Retinitis Pigmentosa awareness.

In college and as a recent college grad, I competed in several biathlons and a triathlon. I put an awful lot of miles on my bike in those early years, riding after work and on weekends for the freedom cycling provided. It was exhilarating, and the workout was challenging and satisfying.

But I had not ridden my bike in years (even on a stationary wind trainer). So I asked myself why I kept it. Once again, I was holding on out of nostalgia and selfishness. But once again, I found a way letting go could make a difference.

A friend from our church does bike repairs for a ministry that sells bikes to raise money for children in Jamaica. I donated my bike to the ministry, and my friend fixed it up and sent my wife a picture of the restoration. Giving my bike to this cause brought me more joy than hanging onto it ever could have.

CHAPTER 19

The Giant Bumblebee

International track star and world-record holder Orrville Rogers once said, "I can because I do."

At the age of 101, Orville was still running. He could because he got out and did it. He inspires me. There's a lot I can't do anymore because of my vision loss. But, with an effort, there's a lot of things I can still do. Running is one of them. Although I got rid of several of my toys, I did not get rid of my running shoes.

Running always relaxes me and helps clear my mind and relieve stress. It's one of the few remaining independent activities I can do without any assistance from a white cane or from a person. I live in a community with no curbs or sidewalks, but I can see shades of darkness and brightness, so I run when it's sunny and I can see the contrast between the pavement and the grass. Our community also is relatively small, so I memorized my route.

In our old subdivision, where we lived for 20 years, there were no sidewalks, either. But the streets were wide with a painted white line four feet off the curb that provided a grid-like boundary to be used as a sidewalk. When I ran, I could use the concrete curbside as a visual guide because it stood out against the black asphalt street. I also could feel the painted white line with the bottoms of my feet.

I would run a few miles during the day, when fewer cars drove through the subdivision. I thought this was a pretty safe bet — until one day I was introduced to a Buick with a bear-hug and a kiss on the cheek. I rolled over the hood and landed in someone's front yard.

I quickly checked myself for broken bones and cuts. Finding none, I slowly got to my feet and collected my composure. I realized the passenger's side of the Buick was nearly driven up onto the concrete curbside. No one had come out of the car yet, and I was sure this was going to be a hit-and-run. I thought as soon as I stood to my feet the driver would realize I was alive and drive away. But instead, the driver's-side door finally opened and an elderly man stepped out of the car.

As the man made his way toward me, he appeared to be shaking and had quivering lips. I fully expected him to apologize and ask if I was all right. He didn't. He yelled at me for getting in his way. No kidding. A real live "Mad Max: Beyond Thunderdome" hits me then chews me out. What brazen audacity. I found the old man and his stance absolutely silly. I wanted to tell Mad Max to go pound sand, but I actually felt sorry for the guy. I realized, like me, he was probably fighting for his independence. I remembered what it was like to come to terms with giving up my car, and I knew this man probably had issues of his own to come to terms with. So, when he finished his rant, I calmly responded, "Don't worry about it." I brushed myself off and took in a deep breath. I prayed to overcome the fear of that hair-raising experience, and I prayed for the old man, too. I located my visual guide along the curbside and continued my run.

The whole time, I couldn't stop wondering how the man could not have seen me.

I tried to convince my wife this incident was a one-off and nothing like it would ever come close to happening again. She placed an online order for a runner vest for me to wear anyway.

During my daily runs, I now wear a bright, neon yellow runner vest with very large black capital letters that spell BLIND across the front and back. Everything about this vest draws attention to me. It says to drivers: "Hellooo! See me because I may not see you!" We felt confident it would do the trick.

Well, I couldn't believe it, but a few months later — while wearing the vest — I was run off the road in a near-hit.

I was on a morning run inside the walking-lane. When I came to a bend in the road, I looked up ahead and, even with my poor vision, I noticed a car-shaped object barreling down the hill directly toward me. I narrowly escaped the collision when I dove into a lawn. My adrenaline was pumping. Elderly driver or not, I jumped to my feet and yelled — intently and with sincerity — some friendly, profanity-laced phrases thanking the speeding driver for testing my quick reflexes and agility.

A bystander who witnessed the episode mentioned the distracted driver was on a cell phone.

My thoughts began to race. What the heck is going on here? I look like a giant bumble bee running alongside the road. What is the problem? Why is this vest not alerting drivers to pay attention? What do they want from me?

As I resumed my run, I was struck with an analogy. With the shoe on the other foot, I wondered if God had once asked me the same question. I suddenly realized God had been wearing a neon yellow vest for years, trying to draw my attention. He was saying, "Hellooo! I'm here! I've blessed you over and over again! What else do you want from me?" And for years, I had ignored him.

I've had numerous near misses with cars over the years I've been running. I have to constantly be aware of my surroundings as best I can, with or without a bright yellow vest. But I praise God for the years of good health and continued athletic ability he has given me even into my late 50s. I often think about Orrville Roger's world record. I have many years yet before I can compete in his age bracket, but it would be cool if it turns out I still have the good health to go after that record as a blind man. Who knows? We'll see what happens when I get there.

In the meantime, I praise God for every stride I take during my daily runs, and I would be perfectly content if the next stride taken should be my last. Until then, I'll continue to enjoy running. Like Orville, "I can because I do."

Chapter 20

The Final Phase

With the ability to work from home came the ability to work at any time. If there were major technical issues anywhere around the world, day or night, it was my responsibility to tend to them until there was a resolution. I was working on one of these stressful and difficult issues one night when I had an awakening that the end of my professional career was near.

As I sat at my computer, I began to notice details on my monitor, such as text, were vanishing from my center view. I was accustomed to losing my peripheral vision and having to daily adjust to a new visual field, but missing my center vision was new. I scheduled an appointment with my ophthalmologist to find out what was happening.

At age 45, my remaining peripheral vision was so small the ophthalmologist couldn't even measure it. The disease was entering its final phase.

Like a hungry parasite, Usher Syndrome Type II devoured my entire peripheral vision and still wasn't satisfied. It turned its attention to the prime choice center area of my retina — the macula — to sate its appetite. It was salivating to complete its mission.

My wife and I prayed over the options left on the table. Option 1 was to do nothing and contemplate retirement. Option 2 was to have surgery to remove the cataracts in both eyes, which had been caused by my damaged retinas. Option 2 held the possibility I could extend my professional career and see my family a bit longer. There was nothing to lose in this final phase, so the decision to have the surgery was an easy decision to make.

The operations would take place one eye at a time, two weeks apart. I asked my surgeon if he had ever operated on someone with Usher Syndrome. He said I was his first, but he assured me he had performed thousands of these operations. He explained the process of removing the cataract and implanting a new artificial lens. For most patients, sight was restored within the next couple of days.

With that assurance, I took only one day off from work for the surgery. It turned out, however, recovery for someone with Usher Syndrome took about a week.

Although excruciatingly challenging, I went back to work the day after surgery and worked as if it were my last day. I wore a patch on one eye and used my other eye to read. My nose was literally inches away from my computer monitor. I was only able to take so much of the intense eye strain produced from struggling to read my spreadsheets and email messages.

As the days progressed, my wife and I were extremely concerned that none of my sight would be restored.

Finally, once the swelling in my eye receded, my limited central vision began to return — but not without a difficult adjustment.

The post-surgery recovery experience of that first eye was absolutely huge, quite literally.

The kitchen sink looked as large as a bathtub and door knobs looked as large as tire rims. I felt claustrophobic for days while my brain worked to adapt to the new lens and visual field. The increased challenges had me thinking the surgery was a very bad decision. I wondered if the results were too drastic for my eyes, and I had no clue how to deal with it.

Frustration and fear set in as I waited for the surgery on my second eye. It overwhelmed me at times and required me to seek calm and patience.

It wasn't until after the second surgery and recovery I began to experience some new changes in my vision. With both eyes working together, the clarity, richness and boldness of colors materialized. It had been so long since I had seen colors in that way, I had forgotten what they truly looked like. They had been shrouded in the cataracts' haze.

I wanted to reach my hand into the TV screen and dip my finger in the colors to feel them and to taste them. I frequently stopped when walking around the neighborhood so I could take in the world with my new vision. It had incredible crispness and clarity. I recall staring at the bark on a tree one morning, marveling in its simple beauty.

However, I knew the removal of the cataracts would not remove my disease. It would remove some of the cloudiness from my center vision, but it would not repair the damaged eye tissue of my retina.

Time passed. Then, one evening as I stood in front of a mirror preparing to brush my teeth, I noticed something odd, yet familiar. I moved my face closer to the mirror and squinted my eyes, trying to focus on my facial features. Something was wrong. No, it wasn't my ugly mug that was odd. It was that, once again, the details were hazy. I could barely see the shape of my eyes, nose, mouth and ears. Once again, I headed to my ophthalmologist to find out what was going on.

CHAPTER 21

The Final Lap

I was determined to fight for every last bit of vision available to me so I could continue to work, provide for my family and see my wife and kids. But this disease was equally determined. It hunkered down to take everything away. Eighteen months after the cataract surgery, a secondary cataract had developed in both eyes. I underwent laser eye surgery called YAG to remove the secondary cataracts.

The procedure was non-invasive and took only a few minutes to complete. I expected to regain some improved central vision like I experienced when the cataracts were initially removed. Unfortunately, that would not be the case. Upon a post-op visit with my eye surgeon, he told me the news I didn't want to hear.

"I'm very sorry," he said, after he confirmed the secondary cataract surgery had fully removed the cataracts but not offered any visual improvements. "That's all we can do." Then he turned and walked out of the room.

He was gracious enough not to add salt to the wound by stating the obvious — the disease had continued to degrade my central vision. This I could conclude on my own. From a medical perspective, it was the end of the line. Nothing more could be done. I lowered my head and stared at the floor, absorbing the gravity of the moment.

I was deflated. I began a serious self-evaluation to determine whether to step down from my career. No one at work, including my managers, colleagues and members of my technical team, ever knew the depths of my daily challenges in simply performing my job with ever-diminishing vision. Only my wife knew the level of frustration I was enduring.

Don't misunderstand — I was truly grateful to God for giving me many years of stamina to continue to do the job I loved. But I was tired of trying to work while my degrading vision kept pulling me the other way. I was not bitter about the situation; I was just done facing the frustrations and challenges every day. I felt like I just completed a 12 and 12 and needed to throw my hands above my head and inhale oxygen. I had neither the energy nor the patience to continue my work, and I knew my sight would continue to worsen.

I worked through the self-evaluation in my mind during a daily run, and it occurred to me maybe my focus and my perspective were all wrong. Helen Keller captured this truth precisely when she was quoted as saying "The only thing worse than being blind is having sight but with no vision".

Maybe I should not measure my levels of tiredness, frustration or deflation to determine the fate of my work. Maybe I should measure my will — my will to suffer and sacrifice; to be persistent and dedicated; to get back on my feet each time I'm knocked down; to maximize my energy; to give everything I've got and never give up; and to overcome, all in the name of Jesus Christ. How strong was my will to give my unconditional trust, faith and commitment to him and to press forward with the goal of performing my work at a high level with my absolute best effort, one day at a time? This was my renewed focus when I decided to take on this trial of life a bit longer.

I also heard a couple of familiar voices in my thoughts who challenged me along the way. I heard my stepfather's encouraging words to hustle: "Hubba! Hubba!" I heard Coach Mentis telling me to keep driving my legs and keep the drive alive. I couldn't turn down a challenge from my mentors. I would keep going, keep pushing forward and rise to what would turn out to be the drive toward my final lap. "Blow the whistle! I'm ready to go!"

I would take the small amount of vision available to me and work another seven years. There were no special tools to help me, so I improvised. I had a desk lamp that shined on my keyboard and, later, bright yellow stickers labeled with bold black letters. I changed my computer settings to create more contrast. The corner of my monitor became home base for my mouse, the point from which I would drag the arrow and follow it closely to the place I needed to be. The efforts proved every bit as exhausting as a 14 and 14 during my high school football summer training.

Nothing comes easy.

CHAPTER 22

The Reunion

I didn't ask for it, but one of my buddies had given me Coach Mentis's phone number. I was in my forties at the time. I think I held onto it for over a year or two, wondering what there was to talk about beyond the usual greetings. Then, one day, I had the urge to take a break from work, and I decided to give Coach Mentis a call.

I dialed his number and he picked up the phone. I felt a bit awkward as I offered my greetings and told him who was calling. Amazingly, after more than 25 years, Coach not only remembered me but called out my full name and football jersey number and named the position I had played all those years earlier. I was stunned. The best I could offer in response was a string of totally unexpected words that just poured out of my mouth.

"I experienced night vision blindness, Coach. That's why I missed that block!" I blurted.

How stupid. I had no idea why I said it. It wasn't like he would even remember. I guess it had weighed heavy on my mind all these years. Even though it was a meaningless point now, a part of me wanted him to know I tried my best despite the unknown vision challenges I was experiencing at the time. I've always felt I never reached my full potential on the field.

There was a moment of silence, then Coach spoke: "Mike, it's alright."

We had a good conversation after that. We talked a bit about our lives, and I filled him in on what was happening in mine. After that phone call, we kept in touch with occasional calls and emails.

We met again face-to-face at our football team's 30-year reunion. The legendary Coach Mentis was 83 at the time and still commanded the utmost respect. I was reliving the glory days with my old teammates when I noticed Coach walking directly toward me. It was like that day on the sideline, but this time I didn't try to avoid him. He reached my side and told me to sit down. We talked privately for a few minutes, and Coach said he knew someone who could heal the blind. He wanted to make sure I was on the path toward Christ. Then he told me to bow my head as he prayed. My wife slipped my sunglasses from the top of my head to cover my eyes as they began to well up with tears. Coach Mentis truly defined what it means to be a coach for life.

The last email I received from Coach Mentis was a message that startled me. It was written in bold, capital letters: **"I AM READY FOR THE GOOD LORD TO CALL ME HOME! I AM READY!"** He knew his time on earth was drawing to a close. I took a knee and lowered my head in prayer. I thanked God for placing him in my life and for all of the lives he had touched.

I hoped I would be able to proclaim my readiness as boldly as Coach when it was my time to go home to the Lord. But now it was time to begin my next step toward regaining independence with the assistance of a white cane.

CHAPTER 23

The Search

Inside my house, I could maneuver around blindfolded. I knew every inch of my home and moved around with ease, but once outside that familiar setting, it was another matter.

To get around outside the house, such as at restaurants, I had been using my wife's elbow. For years, I'd been holding on to her as she escorted me around obstacles to my desired location. She would verbalize what lay ahead and when I needed to take action. She would say things like, "Here's a curb. Step up," or "Duck your head. We are passing under some tree branches." When she wasn't around, my daughters stepped in to guide me. When no one was around, I was on my own to do the best I could.

To protect myself, I developed a Frankenstein-like technique of swinging and swirling my outstretched arms as if swatting flies. I took slow, methodical steps to kick anything in front of me so I didn't stumble or trip. I used this technique when moving around in the yard, garage or driveway. However, to avoid odd looks and questions — and potentially frightening people — I didn't use this method in public.

Of all of the embarrassing incidents I've experienced trying to get around, one stands out in my memory as an all-time low point in my life.

It was a weekday morning, and I had to work from my customer's location rather than from home. I nervously walked through the highly secured entrance of my client's large corporate office. Suddenly, I was stopped dead in my tracks by an unforgiving glass door. My nose wasn't broken, but my lip began to bleed. A security guard took notice and immediately approached me. He removed my security badge and called for backup.

I was quickly escorted to a back room somewhere in the building. I sat in a chair and kept repeating to security I had not been drinking or taking drugs. A company nurse showed up soon after to look after my bleeding lip. She confirmed there was no notable scent of alcohol. Again, I explained why I had walked into the door. Deeply embarrassed and totally humiliated by the entire episode, I just wanted to hide. My badge was returned to me and, to ensure I arrived safely, I was escorted to my assigned office space.

I needed help.

Searching for it was a frustrating process.

When I tried to find some sense of direction on how to safely improve my mobility, I discovered I was disqualified from white-cane training on two state regulatory fronts — I was too young (wasn't over 65 years old) and I earned too much money (I had a job with an income). So, I asked for, and was then given, a phone number for an independent white-cane orientation and mobility trainer. I would be required to pay out-of-pocket for their services. But numerous calls and messages were never returned.

Searching for help on my own seemed a dead end, and the state regulations that disqualified me from that angle seemed absurd. However, the roadblocks turned out to be a Godsend because they led me directly where I was meant to go for help.

CHAPTER 24

The Freedom

My wife began searching the Internet to find mobility help for me. She came across an article featuring a lady from Oxford, Georgia, who had the same eye disease I have (Retinitis Pigmentosa) and who had high reviews of some organization in Rochester Hills, Michigan, called Leader Dogs for the Blind. The article had pictures of this lady walking down her driveway, smiling with a white cane in her hand.

I had not crossed a single street on my own, outside of my subdivision or a parking lot, in more than 10 years. At the age of 50, I was about to learn how to do it as a blind person. For a week, I was given the opportunity to stay in a dorm-type room on the Leader Dogs for the Blind campus and have personalized orientation and mobility training with an expert.

Although I was not at Leader Dogs for a guide dog, there were, obviously, lots of guide dogs all around the facility. I asked a lot of questions about them and quickly learned they were top-gun, hardworking dogs that received highly specialized training for the immense responsibility of guiding the visually impaired and the blind. I was given an opportunity to "test drive" a black Labrador retriever guide-dog-in-training while I was there. Like a kid in grade school with a substitute teacher, this pup sensed I wasn't a trained guide-dog handler. She cut a corner across the grass while guiding me, and my trainer quickly corrected her. We completed our walk and, despite the mischief, I was in awe of this pup and all the dogs at the facility. I knew immediately where I was going when the time was right for that next step. Until then, I'd be learning to use a white cane to guide myself.

The positive impact of O&M training was immediate. I quickly established what I was still capable of doing and how I could move independently. By noon on Monday, which was my first day, I had learned to cross a busy street and was feeling confident and motivated. The wind was full in my sails, and I was eager to learn more as every day brought increased goals and challenges.

By the end of the week, I had learned how to confidently maneuver around obstacles and locate and climb up and down stairs. I put in miles and miles of walking and accomplished crossing several four-lane highways on my own.

How does a blind man cross a highway without getting killed? It can be a hair-raising experience, especially when the sounds of roaring engines are blowing by at high speeds. I learned to use things like the warmth of the sun on my face, the wind, the coolness of the shade and surrounding noises to orient myself while I walked several blocks and crossed streets completely blindfolded. Practicing this in total darkness helped me learn to use all the resources at my disposal to ensure my safety while maneuvering independently.

I especially need all those resources when crossing a highway. I know I'm at an intersection when my white cane meets the truncated domes or tactile pavings on the curb ramp. Before crossing, I prepare myself with information about my surroundings. I listen to the flow of traffic on the street parallel to me and the street I'm to cross. Hearing when each street seems quiet and when cars are whizzing by helps me discern the traffic-light cycles. Once I've gathered my information, I locate the pedestrian crosswalk signal and press the button. I move back to the curb and line up my feet at the edge of the ramp with my feet pointed in the direction I will travel. The last thing I do before crossing is listen for idling engines, which signals the vehicles have come to a stop. Then, with my white cane out in front of me to ensure drivers have noticed me, I continue my walk in a straight path to meet the curb on the other side, safe and sound.

My training experiences were gratifying, and my confidence soared as I became more self-sufficient. But something was nagging at me.

One day during a break, I shared with my O&M instructor a story I had heard about a married couple.

The husband had developed macular degeneration, then lost his job. From time to time he could be found wandering around his neighborhood, carrying grocery bags or to-go boxes from a local restaurant, trying to find his way back home. One time, the paramedics were called because the man was found bleeding on the curbside. He had taken a fall that left him with a nasty gash on his head.

The man's neighbors began to ask the obvious question: Where was his wife?

It turned out even though they were living under the same roof, they had recently separated, and she had refused to help him in any way, including preparing meals. Some of the neighbors heard about this and brought home-cooked meals to the man so he could eat without leaving his house.

The man became a heavy drinker and later died. The entire series of events took place within a few short years.

"I've heard those sad stories a hundred times and it doesn't surprise me" my O&M instructor responded. "Unfortunately, far too often, married couples break their wedding vows when a spouse becomes sick or disabled, and then they file for divorce. They want out."

"Wow," I thought. Her response stunned me. I thought the story I told was a rarity. It was not, and that concerned me. I began to wonder why my wife and I did not resemble that story.

I realize now there is a stark contrast between how easy it can be for couples to stick together during good days and how difficult it can be for couples to stick together during days of challenges.

When I think about the early days of my marriage, it was easy for my wife and me to stick together because we were in good health and didn't have any real struggles or sufferings to speak of. A lot sure had changed since then. I was there at Leader Dogs for the Blind for white-cane training, which was a place far removed from the days of good vision and far removed from the altar where my wife and I stood and spoke our wedding vows.

My wife did not get a pass to ignore the struggles of my diminishing eyesight. It has been painful for her to watch the disease unfold and to witness my suffering. I have a significant health issue that has a significant impact on my wife's life, as well. Unfortunately, she also did not get a pass to ignore me when I wasn't the most pleasant blind guy to be around. Today, I'm more mindful of how I handle my struggles, knowing it has a direct impact on my wife and our marriage.

But I've not always been successful in holding my tongue. I've not exactly welcomed tripping and falling with a smile and open arms. Instead, I've used a few choice words to release my feelings. One night, Becky had to listen as I loudly expressed my frustration on the ride home from a noisy and dark restaurant where we had gathered with two other couples. I was, essentially, a statue in a chair, feeling the weight of total isolation from the group, unable to converse with anyone in any way. Yet my wife still soldiered through our marriage with me.

What personal cost is one spouse willing to pay for the sake of their marriage? What kind of person would make the sacrifices required? A person with character. Andy Stanley, in his book "Louder Than Words," defined character as "the will to do what is right, as defined by God, regardless of personal cost." My wife has certainly personified that definition. This is one of the valuable lessons I have learned since having that conversation with my O&M instructor.

My week of intensive training came to an end, and it was time to board the plane and head home to Atlanta. I stepped inside the cabin of a commercial airline jet with my white cane leading the way. The freedom the cane provided, the burden it lifted, brought back my playful sense of humor and gave me the power to joke about my situation. So when I was greeted by a couple of flight attendants, I couldn't help responding with: "Hi there. My name is Mike and I'm your pilot. Can you help me find the pilot's seat please?" We all laughed.

My cane was telescopic, and I was able to fold it up and put it out of the way when it was not in use. This was very handy, especially in making a grand entrance when I arrived home. I walked in and unfurled my white cane in front of my wife and kids for the first time. In that moment, I thought about the huge change this cane represented. Having a white cane was not a change only for me but for my family as well. This would be a positive new normal. My wife and children would no longer need to lead me around while I held one of their elbows or hands.

In fact, the white cane proved helpful for all of us in some cases where I led my family instead of the other way around. People sure clear the way when they see a white stick coming at them, swinging like a sickle with a full head of steam. In a way, I felt like a fullback again, clearing a running lane. It was kind of nice.

One Sunday morning, my wife asked if I would mind if she stopped by the grocery store to pick up a few items on our way home from church.

"Of course I don't mind," I said. "But I'm coming in with you."

A hilarious episode ensued — well, I thought so, anyway.

I was once again in a playful mood. I admit, they weren't really a rarity these days. Once we stepped inside the store, my inner child took over. I stood at the end of the shopping cart begging my wife to push and give me a ride. Then I started swiping my white cane from side to side down the aisle, clearing people out of the way and making loud noises as the cane hit the baseboard of the metal shelves.

I drove my wife absolutely crazy. Embarrassed to be seen with me any longer, she hurriedly grabbed the few items she needed and made a mad dash toward the checkout. As she loaded the groceries onto the conveyor belt, the cashier asked my wife the standard question: "Were you able to find everything you needed?" I stood across the conveyor belt from the cashier. Holding my white cane in front of me, I answered for my wife: "I couldn't find anything I needed."

I thought Becky's head would complete a 360-degree turn like an owl and devilish horns would emerge from her scalp. Instead, she quickly paid the cashier and literally sprinted out of the exit doors, leaving a trail of dust across the parking lot. I didn't know she could move so fast. I calmly grabbed the remaining shopping bags from the checkout counter, slipped on my sunglasses and began to walk toward the exit with my white cane leading the way. I was somewhere in the middle of the parking lot heading in the general direction of our parked car when I heard a voice behind me.

"Excuse me. Can I help you with anything?"

I must have looked pathetic wearing my sunglasses and holding bags of groceries in one hand and a white cane in the other. To any onlooker, I was aimlessly wandering through the parking lot. It was an awfully kind gesture for this man to offer, but I couldn't pass up the opportunity to play this. "Sure," I said. "I'm looking for my car so I can drive home."

CHAPTER 25

The Perfect Plays

B esides the independence gained from learning to navigate with my white cane, there were other tips and adjustments I adopted from my O&M training that allowed me to gain more independence around my house as my vision continued its decline.

I began to use objects around my home to provide cues to guide me from room to room. Conceptually, I viewed everything that touched the floor as my offensive linemen. The couch, chairs, dressers, walls and tables are my center, guards, tackles and tight ends. Each position (or piece of furniture) has an assigned responsibility in my house, which may change depending on where I'm trying to go. If I line them up properly, the plays called on the field will be executed flawlessly, exactly as designed. Let's try a few plays so I can demonstrate what I'm talking about.

Power I Right 34 is a play to bust through the right guard (kitchen table) and right tackle (wall) to locate the dog bowls. Gliding my hand along one end of the kitchen table will lead me to a wall, and I use a stiff-arm off that wall to reach down to the dog bowls. Perfectly executed play.

Another great play is T Formation 31 Dive, which is used when I need to get to the bathroom in the middle of the night. Now that I'm in my 50s, having an urgent need to empty my bladder during the night is not uncommon, so this is a no-nonsense, quick bang-bang play right up the gut with no wasted movements. It is executed between my center (dresser) and my left guard (wall). I simply glide my hand along the edge of my dresser, which leads me directly to the master bathroom. I find the wall with a stiff arm, then cut hard to the left to the toilet. Perfectly executed play.

Perhaps my favorite play is Wing T Unbalanced Jet Sweep Left. I run toward the left side of the line while my left tight end (kitchen table), my left tackle (wall) and my left guard (wall) all block down so I can find my La-Z-Boy recliner. I glide my hand along the edge of the kitchen table then bounce off to the left and glide my hand along the wall. With a stiff-arm here and a side-step there, I cut to the right wall, which leads me to the back side of my recliner in the living room. To move to the front of the recliner requires a quick spin move, then I sit down and kick up my feet. Nicely done.

My moves around the house are as sweet as the famous NFL Hall of Fame running back Sweetness Walter Payton. Well, in my dreams, but you get the idea. The whole purpose is to avoid objects safely and gain independence.

My family contributes, as well, by pushing in their chairs at the table and putting away shoes so I am not unexpectedly tackled. I apply this basic concept to other areas around my home, such as the garage and even organizing the refrigerator so I know where to find things easily.

I made adjustments outside my house, as well. One of them involved mowing the lawn. I placed a large, bright object on either end of the row of grass I intended to cut, then kept my vision focused on the object and aimed for it the best I could as I pushed the mower. Other things didn't require a visual cue. Angry red fire ants have a way of letting the blind guy know they don't appreciate him standing on their house. I'd rather catch yard darts any day than be bitten by a hoard of red ants.

I have no doubt my mowing left behind beautifully man-icured Mohawk patterns of uncut grass throughout the yard. But hey, that was okay by me. Imperfect, but it got the job done, and it was worth the effort.

That's what matters to me — the effort I put in to keep trying to accomplish things as normally as possible while losing my sight. Orrville Rogers' quote "I can because I do" is something I continue to try to live out. I may never break his world record. Heck, I'll be lucky to be alive at his age. I may never have a nice and even cut yard, either, but I vow to never stop doing.

Chapter 26

The Dry Levee

When thinking about our futures and retirement, most of us like to be in the driver's seat. We want to call the shots, and we feel comfortable we can predict our future to a certain degree. We intend to time our retirement according to our own will, somewhere around typical retirement age, but sometimes it doesn't work out the way we plan.

It didn't for me.

I did not take advice from medical professionals — or advice from anybody, for that matter — when determining when to call it quits. But my self-evaluation had resurfaced. There were two indicators by which I chose to measure myself: 1) Have I lost the ability to perform my most basic job functions? and 2) What does my heart say — do I know in my heart the time has come to stop working? When the answer to both of these questions was yes, I would know the time had come to end my professional career.

And so it came to pass.

In late 2016, my company initiated a large-scale reduction in our workforce. As a manager, I had reviewed the layoff list. It was large, and as I went through the names, I knew it was time. It would be selfish to hold onto a position I was far from capable of continuing while the company laid off someone else who would be able to perform the job for years to come. I decided to add my own name to the list so someone else's job would be saved..

Having come to that conclusion, I left it all on the field, and my heart carried no regrets. Years of working with persistence, perseverance, focused dedication and passion for my career, company, clients and family was nearing the finish line, but I knew in my heart I had given my best and worked in a manner to honor Christ every day. I was thankful to Him for giving me the hope and desire to pursue the opportunity of a lifetime, and each morning I woke up and got out of bed, I gave it my all. I also knew it was OK to accept the inevitable had arrived and it was time to step down. It was a good run.

I had enjoyed and thrived on the challenges my company provided me. I would often ask my managers to assign me to the toughest project available. They usually took me up on my offer, like the time I was assigned to a high-pressure, beast of an account from which the three previous people had resigned. Two had stepped down within six months of taking the position, and the third resigned after a year, when he suffered a heart attack. Although that concerned me initially, I was not one to back down. Though it proved formidable, I loved the challenge and served on that account for more than five years.

Now, things were different. With my enormous stubbornness, I wanted to believe I could still perform at the highest level, but I couldn't.

With much prayer, thought and preparation, I volunteered to be laid off, ending my career. I retired at the age of 53. It was hard to accept the reality of a long chapter coming to a close sooner than I'd planned. It was like a favorite TV show getting canceled before the series finale.

I don't know why, but Don McLean's "American Pie" lyrics played in my thoughts.

"I started singin' bye, bye Miss American Pie, drove my Chevy to the levee but the levee was dry."

It was as if my own levee had gone dry ... in this case, in both eyes. Despite that feeling, I was confident I could move forward in strength and peace because I had spent years building what I perceived to be a bullet-proof faith in Christ.

Then I was presented with another unexpected surprise.

Within a few weeks of my retirement, I was blindsided by a body slam to the ground that took the breath from my lungs and left me exasperated.

I looked over my shoulder to see what in the world had knocked me off my feet. Coming into view was the massive storm I thought had long since passed. It had circled back and returned like a bounty hunter. It was dead on my tracks. I couldn't stop the gravitational pull toward depression.

I was now unable to drive, unable to visually see my wife's and kids' facial features and unable to perform my job, but if I thought things couldn't get any worse, I needed to think again, and I needed to dig deeper in my faith. The disease was far from finished.

My kids were in high school and college. My wife had returned to the professional workforce full time and the house was empty and deadly quiet. I walked into my home office at the end of the hall. It once had the appearance of a busy mini datacenter complete with computer hardware and equipment glowing with dancing, flashing lights and emitting a monotonous humming. Now it resembled a graveyard.

There on my desk were the remains of my once whirring office. Phones that rang continuously now rested in complete silence. All the voices from around the world heard during all those team and client phone calls and hours of meetings had all subsided. Monitors, laptops, keyboards and servers lay dark, cold and still.

I sat down at my desk to reflect on the years of work I had done here. I was no doubt mightily grateful to have had the opportunity to work 18 years doing what I truly loved for an amazing company. But I didn't realize how deeply entrenched in my work I had become. Life up to that time had been full of adjustments, but no longer working was going to be one of the toughest adjustments of all. The decision to retire, although necessary and unavoidable, was like crashing after a rush of adrenaline. I felt like I had completed the final sprint of a marathon and immediately collapsed after crossing the finish line. Like the abrupt brush of wind felt from a passing semi truck, my career had sped by and now was over. The finality was sobering and left me empty. The pieces of my identity and purpose that were tied into work no longer existed.

Who was I now? What was I supposed to do? "This can't be where it ends, can it?" I asked myself.

For the first time, I didn't have a job. I no longer provided an income to support my family. There'd be no more calls from coworkers who sought my advice, counsel and assistance because of my skills and experience. 60 to 100-hour work weeks screeched to a halt, and I had nothing but time. I was lost. The weight of it all began to set in.

Compounding my internal thoughts were echoes of the questions and remarks I heard when people learned I was ending my career. I must have fielded the same questions 10,000 times. "What are you going to do now, Mike?" "What will you do with all your time?" I also was the recipient of uninvited comments that left a lasting sting. "We were put on this earth with the purpose to work." "I don't know if I can ever stop working; I will have to do something."

Although the remark about purpose may be true, it implied if I no longer was employed in my career field I no longer had purpose or I was worthless. The comments of naysayers swirled around in my mind.

As if through a loudspeaker, the storm replayed over and over again the message that I now was just a useless blind man who was no longer needed and had no real purpose. I was challenged to answer a question: "What do you have left to offer?" I had trouble answering because what I believed to be my last remaining source of significance, my ability to independently provide any direct contribution, had just been shut down. I remember thinking to myself, "Now that I'm here Lord, where am I to go?" I didn't know then, but a new path would emerge. It just required time to develop.

Although I could feel the undertow tugging me toward the sea of depression, I did not panic. But I also did not take it lightly. I hunkered down and made a commitment to remain unwavering in my faith in God. This storm was tough, and I had not anticipated how difficult the detoxification process would be as my work identity began to unravel and a new identity slowly surfaced. But as I weathered this storm with faith, God began to change me, and I was able to reflect on things from a different viewpoint.

God took me back to that Sunday years before when I heard the pastor's off-script message, and then to a few months later when I was saved. What an unbelievable ride my life had been since that time. I realized God had his hand on me long before I knew it. I had taken many small steps forward during my walk with Christ in those years, so I sat down and started writing down every unanticipated moment. These words became my profession of faith, which I had the opportunity to share when I took the significant, bold step forward to get baptized.

My church liked people to write a short synopsis of their faith journey before their baptism. The stories were turned into 5-minute videos for the congregation to view just before the actual baptism took place. I sent the profession of faith I had written to the videographer. She shared it with the ministry team and later called me to ask if they could create a longer-form video of my faith story to accompany a sermon series they were developing on life's challenges, then tape a summary version to accompany the baptism. I was surprised, but of course God had already planned how my story would be used for his glory.

The message God led me to share at the milestone of my baptism can be found at the end of this book, and I hope you take it to heart. I never anticipated a lot of things in my life, and I certainly never anticipated I would be baptized. But as I stood waiting to be dunked in the pool of water where my sins would be symbolically washed away and I would publicly profess my belief in Jesus as my savior, I was filled only with joy. I asked God to allow my faith in Christ to lead me the final 20 feet to the pool to complete this long journey. As I stepped to the edge, I said, "Get out of my way because I'm going to be baptized today!"

CHAPTER 27

The Levee Refilled

As a young man in the workforce, I remember thinking how I couldn't wait to retire. I thought of how great it would be to sit on my backside on a white sandy beach and do a whole lot of nothing. Those thoughts all changed when I read "Half Time," by Bob Buford. I read this book several times, and it changed my perspective on what I would look forward to doing when the time for retirement came.

I realized sitting on a beach might be fun for a few days, but I honestly didn't think I could do that for days on end. There was so much more to do that would be impactful and fulfilling.

Now retired, I needed to find a new purpose. I needed to refill my levee. I adjusted my life to focus on replacing my passion to work and serve through my company with a passion to work and serve in a different capacity — through my church.

My wife and I got involved with serving on the financial ministry team. We used the principles from Dave Ramsey's Financial Peace program to help people become good stewards of the finances God has entrusted to them. I had been blessed by the simple, practical teachings of personal financial responsibility from the best person I ever knew — my stepfather. I'd also been blessed by lessons learned through my own life experiences. What better opportunity to share this knowledge God allowed me to gain with others who may want to learn the importance of budgeting, spending wisely, saving for a rainy day and investing for their future?

Serving in this one new way made me excited to see where God might open more opportunities as we continued to serve.

I have found in the act of serving one another, something incredible happens to the server along with the recipient of the service. You get filled up. My levee was no longer dry.

CHAPTER 28

The Extraordinary

"If the good Lord asked if he could give me a perfectly normal child or Johnny, I'd pick Johnny every time. No doubt about it." – Gene Stallings, former University of Alabama football coach.

This quote reminds me of the unconditional love and determined commitment I saw in my mother throughout my life. You might wonder about her take on raising two sons with a rare disease and not knowing what it's impact might be on their lives. I cannot attempt to answer for my mother, but she sent me the following email after I shared with her the transcript from my baptism. I believe her letter captures her heart in the matter:

Michael John,

This is an outstanding letter. I'm so proud of you. You have such determination. I'm so glad that you got baptized. I'm at a loss for words. I was very moved. I have always been very proud of you. You never let your problem stop you. You and Paul worked extra hard for everything you earned.

You have a very nice life as a result of being so determined. I tried to do what I could to help. I'm so glad you married Becky. She and the girls have been so kind and helpful. I'm proud of you all.

Love
Mom

A cancerous tumor was discovered in my mother's brain soon after she struggled to type and send this last email. Ma passed away on a Saturday morning in April 2018.

Ma was my hero, my inspiration and an incredible pillar of strength. She was an awesome mother who had a heart of gold. She loved to laugh, despite the numerous and extraordinary challenges that came her way throughout her life. She always pressed forward somehow.

Doctors informed her that her sons had severe hearing loss and advised her to place her boys in an institution. She, along with dad, said no. She pressed forward.

She was left alone to raise three children under the age of 10 when she became a widow at the age of 32. She pressed forward.

Doctors informed her that her sons had a profound debilitating disease called Usher Syndrome Type II and we would lose our sight. She pressed forward.

She became a widow for a second time at the age of 62. She pressed forward.

She was diagnosed with parathyroid cancer and skin cancer and recovered from surgery. She pressed forward.

She was diagnosed with cataracts and recovered from surgery. She pressed forward. She was diagnosed with breast cancer and recovered from surgery. She pressed forward.

She was diagnosed with a brain tumor. Though she died while recovering from surgery, she pressed forward till her last breath.

If that's not infused by God's grace, then I don't know what is.

Even when life was difficult, my mother woke up and got out of bed to experience the joy and grace and richness of life God provided. She never brought attention to herself but cared for and served her family and brought humor to those around her.

If someone had asked Ma how she would characterize herself, she would probably say she was just an ordinary person. But I would say she was a person who made ordinary look extraordinary.

Ma didn't read how-to books or receive training on how to raise children as a widowed mother or attend a seminar on how to raise boys with severe hearing loss. No one told her the way to react to the discovery of her son's debilitating disease. She learned in the fire and somehow figured it out and did it right. She worried often, but she also prayed often. She got upset occasionally, but never showed panic. She simply pressed forward in an extraordinarily graceful fashion.

Ma was always there to provide attention and support for her children while we were growing up. She played catch football and baseball with me in the backyard, and we talked about a variety of things, even things a father would normally talk about with his son. She did a fabulous job filling the gap.

Ma was my biggest cheerleader as she rooted for me at every ball game or track meet I participated in. Her words of affirmation were with me every step of the way. There are no words to describe how much that meant to me.

During the course of her life, she experienced the joys of her children graduating from high school and college, her children getting married and holding her grandchildren and great-grandchildren in her arms.

She was there for at least three of my buddies, who called her their second mother, when they needed someone to listen while they talked through difficult moments. She offered them compassion and encouragement.

Equally as important as all of these actions was what she did not do. My mother did not intervene to compensate for my disability. She did not prevent failures from taking place or cushion the many falls. She did not overly protect or shelter me to the point of creating an unhealthy dependency where I would have expected to be rescued whenever I demanded it.

Ma never said, "No, you can't" or "No, you shouldn't." On the contrary. She provided the right balance of nurturing and stepping out of the way to allow me to find my own boundaries. If I didn't fall down and learn to get back up, how would I have learned the unique solutions I needed? Each obstacle I encountered, each failure, became a building block of my life success.

Ma's approach to our disease is what created determination, courage and the independence we needed to stand on our own feet. Ma figured it out, and God certainly equipped her with strength and used her to touch our lives and the lives of many.

But my mother had her struggles, as well.

She struggled mightily as she unnecessarily carried guilt for passing Usher Syndrome Type II to me and my brother. She apologized to me multiple times over the years and, as a parent with children of my own, I have come to understand her point. No parent wants to watch their children suffer. I've always responded to her with the truth, assuring her everything was alright and it was never her fault. She was blameless; she certainly didn't pass on the disease knowingly. I told her I had been blessed in more ways than I ever thought possible through Christ. I am content in my circumstances and I have everything I need. If she only knew how much it pained me to watch her beat herself up with remorse.

One day, my mother watched a pre-recorded video that was aired at my friend's father's funeral. The video featured a mustard seed and my friend's father saying he had a goal for just one person in the sanctuary watching his video to profess their faith and commit their life to Christ as their savior. That video stirred up Ma's curiosity, and she began asking questions, attempting to understand the meaning of "being saved." Over the next few months, it was the focus of our weekly phone conversations. I answered her questions as best I could. Then one day she said to me, "I want to be saved."

"Huh? Now?" I asked.

"Yes," she replied

I was caught off guard. It never occurred to me my mother would ask me to lead her in a prayer of salvation. I also was somewhat new in my faith journey, and I had never done this before. But God prepared me for this awesome moment he had given me. I read Romans 10:9-10 with my magnifying glass to ensure I read it correctly. Then Ma professed Christ as her savior and we prayed together. Just like that, Ma was saved.

My mother lived in a historic home built in the late 1800s in Vermilion, Ohio. It was a home that withstood many Nor'easter storms, where she dwelled in prayer during the nights, where she raised her kids, cooked meals and broke bread with family and friends. It was a home where her first husband passed away, where she married her second husband in the backyard on the shores of Lake Erie and where he also passed away. It was a home of peace, love and joy and a place of refuge. It was a home where she watched beautiful sunrises and sunsets for nearly 50 years.

Ma endured a great deal and also experienced great joy in her life. She was a courageous mother who put aside her pain and provided words of encouragement to her children, reminding us how proud she was of us right up through her last email. She had an incredibly positive influence on those around her.

While in hospice at the end of her days, I kneeled down at her bedside, and my last words to her before she went home were an echo of the encouragement she'd given me my whole life. "I'm proud of you, Ma. You did an awesome job raising us kids. I'm so proud of you. I love you."

CHAPTER 29

The Lightning Rod

There was barely time to mourn my mother's passing when my trusty pal and four-legged companion, Vidalia, passed soon after.

Vidalia was our family dog, a Golden Retriever. She lived to be 11 years old. I still remember the day we picked her out. We took our shoes off at the door of the breeder's home and, while my wife and our young daughters took a seat in the chairs, I sat on the floor. A few minutes later, all of the Golden Retriever puppies woke from their nap and were brought to us still in a sleepy daze — except for one pup. Her head perked up and we made eye contact. Her little legs galloped her stubby fluff-ball body across the room, where she stopped at the end of my feet and bit right into my big toe. That was all it took.

"We'll take this one," I said.

From the day we brought her home, Vidalia wasted no time gaining the run of the house and claiming her territory. She often could be found standing or lying on top of the kids' plastic picnic table on the back patio, and any unmanned stuffed animal was obviously a toy meant for her. For the next several years, she would be crowned the queen who refused to be dethroned.

As she grew, she picked out her furniture. She started in the living room, where she chose a nice, comfortable, leather La-Z-Boy recliner, which had belonged to me. It was mine no longer. I'm such a pushover. She moved to the bedrooms and picked out her favorite bed ... which was all of them, and she moved from one bed to another during the night. We were all pushovers. It was apparent we didn't adopt her, but she adopted us. It seemed the moment she bit my toe was the moment she realized we were easy prey. She gave us her beautiful puppy looks and said: "You all belong to me. You can take me home now." There is no doubt in my mind she preyed upon us.

Vidalia was a fully charged lightning rod who maximized her day in and out of the house.

Inside the house, she somehow got the idea she'd help out with some chores. One day I found her standing on the open door of our dishwasher cleaning the dishes and utensils. She kept the floor completely clean of all crumbs by mopping them up with her tongue, and she made sure all of the food on the countertops and tabletops were put away "properly." She ate sub sandwiches, raw cookie dough, lunch meat, chocolate chip pumpkin muffins and a few hot, oven-baked chicken breasts. She did such a good job, it seemed every time we turned around something was missing, never to be found again.

She ran through my legs like they were an obstacle course and would purposely hit my button to command immediate attention. The button I'm referring to is below my belt. If I had the audacity to hold a standing conversation with my wife or kids, Vidalia would not be ignored. No kidding — like a well-trained bottlenose dolphin hitting a target, she managed to hit my button so many times over the years that she had me doubled over to the point where I used my hands as protective gear.

At 8 p.m. every evening, she would stand in front of me and stare directly at me, purposely blocking my view of the TV so I would get up from the couch. This meant one thing — it was time to wrestle. And that is what we did. She had high energy and loved to attack my kneecaps or elbows, and she tore me up. But when I would grab her up like a baby, she had no defense. I would let her down, dash to open the back door, and we would go outside so she could run laps around the edge of the large, fenced back yard.

She also loved to do what we referred to in the family as the trust fall. She would turn her back to me while sitting next to me on the couch and slowly fall backward onto me and rest her head on my chest. She was as much a lover as she was a fighter.

When it was time for bed, Vidalia followed my wife and kids upstairs. One night I found her sleeping on her back with all four legs pointed straight up toward the ceiling and her head on a pillow, while my daughters were pushed to the side, clinging to the edge of their bed.

With her hilarious personality, it was Vidalia, rather than our human daughters, who turned out to be the rebellious teenager giving my wife and me a challenge. She was defiant when she didn't want to do something, ignoring us or doing the opposite of what she was told. She was a silly, full-of-mischief girl who gave us tremendous joy. She had an amazing ability to make us all laugh and smile. We're very grateful to have had her in our lives.

As you can imagine, under Vidalia's rule there was no question as to whether I could have a guide dog — or any other dog, for that matter. She laid her claim on us, and nothing was going to get in her way.

But after Vidalia's passing, a friend of mine who trains service dogs very directly encouraged me to pursue getting one.

"Stop fooling around, Mike," he said. "You need a guide dog. You'll never regret it." His words would prove to be correct.

CHAPTER 30

The Leader

On September 20, 2017, God created a creature in Iowa with four legs and a tail. He was a Golden Retriever named Fuzz, and he was accepted into the guide dog program at Leader Dogs for the Blind. For the next four months, Fuzz went through intensive training to learn to be a guide dog. Even though we had yet to meet, my bonding process with him began when I learned he was working hard to change my life.

Leader Dogs for the Blind had changed my life once through the Orientation and Mobility training where I learned to navigate my world with a white cane. Now, the organization was changing my life again. Fuzz and I were introduced to each other for the first time in April 2019 in Naples, Florida, where I attended training to accept a guide dog.

Fuzz was an 18-month-old pup who weighed in at 67 pounds and looked like a bashful lion cub. The part in his hair was precisely centered across his handsome, large head. He had four disproportionately huge feet, which anchored his athletic frame, and a barrel chest. His broad shoulders were laced with lean muscles. His body was clearly still filling out.

He came to me with his head lowered and tail nervously swinging back and forth. He sensed it was a big and important moment. I talked to him with a gentle voice and rubbed behind his ears for a few minutes to ease the tension. Later, when I slipped his harness on, he stood at attention with an air of obedience and pride, as if the harness were his superhero cape, and I knew he was going to be an awesome guide.

There were six other clients with me in Naples, who also had traveled from other states to meet and train with their new guide dogs. We all trained and ate meals together. Collectively, we represented a wide range of disabilities and had something in common to talk about. What we learned from one another brought closeness and built friendships. We all had a degree of hearing loss, vision loss or loss of both. Each of us had taken different paths that brought us together for the same reason — to pursue our independence with the use of a guide dog.

Throughout my time in training, I found all the clients to be incredibly motivating and inspiring, and their confidence levels were exceedingly high. I was fascinated and impressed by how well they fully continued to move on with their lives and refused to let vision and hearing loss stop their lives from being full and rich.

During our outdoor training, I was astonished at what Fuzz could do. He stopped at every cross walk, every curb and every set of stairs. He was so amazingly good, with or without his harness, I thought there was something wrong with him. I had never had a dog so obedient and well-behaved. After 11 years of doubling over and gasping for breath from Vidalia hitting below the belt, I could finally relax, stand tall and breathe easy. I was in good hands (or paws, you might say).

As I expected, Fuzz quickly became a rock star. People of all ages would tell me how handsome and beautiful he was and ask if they could pet him.

"Not at this time, because he's working," I politely responded. But I would lower my shoulder and add, "But you can pet me!" They all would laugh, and a few actually took me up on it and patted my shoulder.

When it was time to carry our outside training to the inside, we headed to a crowded mall. Fuzz continued to guide me flawlessly as he whizzed me around crowds of people and in and out of stores. It brought back something I had lost years ago — the freedom of independence that came from simply walking with confidence. What an amazing feeling that was. Then, without my command, Fuzz unexpectedly took a hard left and, with a powerful pull of his harness, led me inside a clothing store. While Fuzz continued to guide me, I realized we were both glancing at clothing articles on display. Very small clothing articles.

"Where are we?" I asked my trainer, who was just behind us to my right.

"You're in Victoria's Secret!"

"Are you pulling my leg?" "No."

"Good boy Fuzz! Good boy!" I smiled. Our bonding process was well underway!

From the day I landed in Naples until the day we completed training, my classmates and I were treated to an amazing experience. The trainers were extremely professional and service oriented. They put in long days and made every effort to assure our comfort and needs were met. Leader Dogs for the Blind had an unbelievably positive impact on my life and those of the other clients, and I can't thank them enough. I also could never fully express my appreciation to all the Leader Dogs donors for their incredible generosity, which makes the program possible.

While in Naples, I had the pleasure of meeting several donors who were able to witness the results of their generosity firsthand as they observed the training program and joined us for dinner one evening. It was a great opportunity for them to see the direct impact of their donations and how their contributions were a game changer in the lives of people like me.

I was thrilled to have Fuzz, who showcased his guiding capabilities for the donors. Fuzz is a cream-of-the-crop guide dog, and I'm so proud of him and of his achievements. He put in the hard work and persistence required to make it through the rigorous training and testing. I'm grateful to have this big boy as my guide in life.

When I brought Fuzz to his new permanent home, he walked in the house and explored with excitement (probably deciding which room he would make his own) and he began to settle in. We both adjusted to his new surroundings and continued to work together and bond. We quickly established our routine of daily walks in the neighborhood and visiting places I frequented regularly. He became familiar with guiding me at home improvement stores, grocery stores, church, doctor's offices and restaurants.

On one exceedingly hot and humid morning, Fuzz and I left the house for our daily walk in the neighborhood, and I decided to leave my hearing aids at home to keep the mics on them dry from my perspiration.

While on our walk, a lady stopped us and immediately began to talk before I had the chance to tell her I'm not much for conversation without my hearing aids. So she continued to talk and talk while I smiled and nodded my head, having no idea what she actually said. I didn't want to appear rude. After several minutes, I realized she was using the word "or." She had asked a question and was waiting for my response. I needed to respond with one option or another, but I had no idea what the question was. I quickly thought how best to respond and surmised that "both" might be the safest. So that's what I said.

The lady was silent for several seconds. There was no reaction, and she was still standing in front of Fuzz and me. This was not a good sign. My response must not have satisfied her question.

"Hold on," I said. "What did you ask me?"

She took a step toward me while I cupped my ears with my palms, then she loudly repeated her question.

"I asked if your dog was a male or a female."

I laughed. I couldn't make this up if I tried.

Today, Fuzz continues to carry himself with rock-star status as he guides me daily.

Everywhere I take him, people say he is a beautiful dog. With or without his harness, he stays by my side just to make sure I'm all right. In addition to being my guide, he is truly a cherished companion, and I make sure he is all right, too.

The Major Shift

S omeone asked me once which of my senses had strengthened to compensate for my vision loss. Many people believe when one sense is diminished other senses are heightened. My not-so-serious response to this person (said with a straight face, of course) was, "my brain."

In all seriousness, it was my sense of smell that was heightened, but something else happened as well.

During my younger years, when I had good vision, I often relied on that vision to compensate for my severe hearing loss. I used my eyes to aid me in everyday activities, such as lip reading, to help me "hear." Later (with the advancement of technology to improve the quality of hearing I have with hearing aids), I began to use my ears to compensate for my vision loss. I sometimes rely on my hearing to get a bearing on my surroundings and communicate with people. This shift was not a surprise, but a normal pattern for someone with Usher Syndrome Type II when, as in my case, the hearing loss remained constant over the years while the vision continued to diminish. Without realizing it, my senses have naturally adjusted to compensate for one another.

Today, I find equipping my ears with the new technology offered by hearing aids is vitally important — now more so than at any other time in my life.

During a follow up visit with an ENT physician who looked after my eardrum, which burst from a nasty fall while water skiing, the doctor said to me, "I have two pieces of good news for you: 1) Your eardrum has fully recovered and healed and 2) you qualify for a cochlear implant."

I never knew my hearing loss was severe enough to qualify for a cochlear implant. It's good to have options on the table when evaluating the best way to improve my hearing, so I put some thought and research into this option over the next several months, but I eventually decided not to pursue the cochlear-implant path.

I made that decision simply because I felt the hearing aids provide me with sufficient amplification, and I have been pleased with the advancements in the technology over my 50 years wearing them.

Thanks to the tremendous competition in the multi-billion dollar hearing-aid industry, companies that produce this equipment jockey for the position of industry leader by manufacturing products with the latest advancements and features. As a result, the capabilities of the modern hearing aid have vastly improved and can produce incredible sound quality.

Today, there are smart hearing aids that use artificial intelligence and Bluetooth for streaming. The technology to provide for my needs and drastically improve my hearing is here, and the advancements keep getting better. However, it does not mean I can show up at an audiologist office, purchase new hearing aids off the shelf, plug them in my ears and I'm good to go. On the contrary, I've gained a lot of experience and knowledge over my many years as a hearing-aid client. I've learned how to communicate my hearing levels to arrive at optimal settings on my equipment. I've become an educated consumer and experienced user and know specifically what I'm after.

Hearing aids typically have to be replaced every seven or eight years. When I'm in the market for new hearing aids, I have learned it is very important to find the right audiologist — one who understands my needs and can find the perfect hearing aids to properly fit my hearing loss.

I have specific criteria I require, at a minimum, to ensure I gain the full benefits of proper configuration, which is the key to achieving the best possible sound quality the hearing aid can offer. For example, I've learned to request a vented hearing aid mold. Without one, my voice sounds very nasal and loud to me, and it drowns out the surrounding sounds. It sounds similar to having water in your ears. I also look for an audiologist who is not tied to a short list of hearing-aid brands. Instead, I look for one who has a wide variety of brands and options to choose from that allow me to find great quality at a price that fits my budget.

Last, and probably most important, is locating an audiologist who not only listens to my needs, but who uses the Real Ear Measurements tool to understand my hearing. The REM tool provides the audiologist with real-time data of what I can and cannot hear while wearing hearing aids (hence the name real ear measurements).

I've had great success when the REM tool is used to configure my hearing-aid settings. This method gives me the proper amplification for my hearing loss. But when not using REM, I have sat witness as audiologists literally read from the manufacturer documentation on how to configure the settings according to my audiogram, all the while having absolutely no idea what I can — or cannot — actually hear.

Audiologists who did not use the REM tool have failed to properly configure my hearing aids 100 percent of the time. I have found myself frustrated and expending a tremendous amount of time on multiple visits, trying to explain the problems while they continue their guesswork. "Did that change help?" they'd ask after fiddling with a few settings. This is the reason many elderly hearing-aid customers give up and don't wear their hearing aids. I don't understand why most audiologists don't use this amazingly helpful tool.

After my most recent hearing-aid purchase, with the settings properly configured, I purchased tickets to a Lauren Daigle concert for my wife and me. As a result of what I've learned to look for in a hearing aid, REM and the vastly improved technology of hearing aids, I was able to experience — with quality and clarity — both the sounds of musical instruments and the God-given beauty of Lauren Daigle's voice. It was like I was hearing her songs for the first time in my life.

CHAPTER 32

The Broken Streak

I hesitated to bring this aspect of my life into focus when writing this book for two reasons: It cuts deep, and the purpose of this book is not to criticize my parents. As easy as it might be to criticize their decisions or actions like a Monday morning quarterback, I'm not here to do that.

On the other hand, these experiences have offered another opportunity to illustrate God's grace is always sufficient and extends to everyone. So here it is.

Over the years, I've heard guys talk about their dads or father figures in a negative or condescending way. They tell stories about what their dads did or didn't do when they were growing up, and they've formed a grudge they will hold for the rest of their lives. Anger and bitterness are wedged deep in their hearts and minds. I was one of those guys, too. The only difference was I didn't talk about my dad. I quietly hated him, and I was certain to take the weight of that burden with me to my grave.

I mentioned in the front of this book my dad was a successful and driven air-traffic controller. Other than that, I don't know much about him. I have only a few fond memories of him, and if there were others, they were over-shadowed by his beatings. I'm not talking about spankings on my backside. I'm talking about hard-core physical abuse. I was afraid of the guy — we all were — and I used to hide when he came home from work. What could I, as a 5-, 6- and 7-year-old kid, have possibly done that was bad enough to justify the level of beatings I received? I don't know. I could understand disciplinary action, but these beatings typically came without warning and seemed to be an extension of rage rather than a reaction to anything I had done. I thought he hated me. I thought he hated our family.

When I picked myself up off the floor after a blow to the head that resulted in a black eye, or after I was decked across the face with such force it lifted me off my feet, that was just another day I couldn't wait to grow up and seek revenge by beating the living crap out of him. As it turned out, I never had the opportunity. My dad passed away when I was still a child.

The fear of his presence came to an end when Ma and I knelt down in front of his casket in 1971. I quietly asked her if I could touch his hand. She nodded. I slowly reached out my arm and softly touched his right hand with a finger, as cautious as if that hand were a snake. I was expecting to jump back to avoid his strike, but his hand didn't move. It was cold. I resented that the opportunity to retaliate, to release my anger on him, was taken away. So I quietly carried a heavy burden of hatred toward my father for years.

In 2016, while having a meal with Ma, we talked about him in some detail, bringing back the memories. She told me she could never leave him. Stunned by her remark, I asked why not. "If he had the slightest hint of me leaving, he would follow through on his threat to take you kids away and disappear to another country without a trace," she said. The fear generated by this threat kept my mother by his side.

This new insight only served to add to the weight of bitterness I carried toward my father. It made me angry that he would have threatened Ma with taking away what was most precious to her. Dad sure left quite a negative mark.

Two years later, as my mother's house was being cleaned out, my dad's wallet was discovered in the attic. It was the closest thing to him in my possession in nearly 50 years. As I held it in my hand, I realized I still had hatred toward the guy, and the vivid image in my mind of beating him senseless in revenge was still alive. I opened his wallet and found three clean and crisp one dollar bills, all dated 1969. I wondered at their significance and thought they might represent each of us kids.

Inside the small compartments of his wallet were several individual pictures of us kids and a couple of Ma. There also were several family pictures. Strange, I thought. This from a guy who hated us? Why would he do that? I had a lot of questions.

While pondering those questions, my mind drifted back in time to riding in the car with a high school buddy. As my buddy was driving, he was constantly pressing the car radio buttons to turn the channel with his fidgety fingers, way before the song was even close to being over, because he was looking for songs he liked.

"How would you know you wouldn't like that song when you haven't listened to it yet?" I had joked.

"Because I just know," he said, and he laughed while continuing to press the radio buttons.

The memory sparked an analogy in my mind.

Each song on the radio represents a person God placed in my life — my friends, mentors, teachers, bosses, grandparents, wife and kids, stepfather, mother and father. Some songs lasted a long time and some were just played for a short time, but each had significance in my life. There's no doubt in my mind each person played their song with their best efforts.

And with their best efforts, all the people in my life have played their songs phenomenally well. All except one: my dad. He played bad music, and I had been quick to press the radio button on my memory of him. I had tuned him out without a thought of listening to his song because, like my buddy, I just knew I wouldn't like it. Then it occurred to me that perhaps instead I could take a few minutes to listen to his song and appreciate his efforts. Maybe he gave his best, but the song he played was not so good because that's how he learned to play. I decided maybe I should be willing to examine this further — and believe me, I was not looking for an excuse to let this guy off the hook.

I think there's truth to the lyrics of the old song "Cat's in the Cradle" by Harry Chapin. In this song, even though the dad didn't spend any time with the son, the son still admires him and says, "I'm going to be like you, dad. You know I'm gonna be like you." As the lyrics continue, the son does grow up to be like his dad, engrossed in his job with little time for family, because that's who he learned to be.

I wondered some more about this and if it was possible what dad inflicted on our family was a generational thing he had learned from his dad when he was growing up. As I came to this realization, I said in my mind, "Hey guys, sorry, but this is my generation and I've decided to snap your streak."

If you took the bad notes out of his music, Dad did make some good decisions. He decided against doctors' advice to stand up for my brother and me, and we were not placed in an institution. He refused that we be treated as disabled and put us back in the public school system to be treated like everyone else. He decided to move the family from Bangkok, Thailand, (he worked there for two years) to a cool house in Vermilion, Ohio, on the shores of Lake Erie. He decided to purchase a boat for the family.

Maybe I was wrong about him. Maybe he didn't hate us. Maybe he tried to play his song well, but just couldn't.

In 2020, I was at home rummaging around for something in my desk drawer when I came across my dad's wallet. I held it in my hand once again. I had done a lot of thinking, listening and more learning over the last couple of years. I may never get over the painful memories Dad inflicted on our family. It certainly never crossed my mind that I should forgive him. After all, I was the innocent bystander. He's not here to apologize to me, so why would I forgive him? As a result, five long decades had ticked away and nothing had changed. In fact, the more I thought about it, I realized I would still carry the burden inside even if I had been able to exact my revenge and give him the beating I had envisioned. The rage inside me would continue, if not worsen, and I would be singing the lyrics: "I'm gonna be like you, dad. You know I'm gonna be like you."

"So where do I go from here?" I thought. There was absolutely no solution that could possibly relieve this burden I carried. None whatsoever ... except for one. Forgiveness.

The Bible mentions the benefits of forgiveness that clearly outweigh the benefits of continuing to carry the hatred I held toward my dad. The passage of time would never release my burden. It was me who needed to change my perspective and forgive him. It was me, the whole time, who needed to take the steps to resolve the burden. Yet another teachable moment for me.

Initially, I thought the lack of my dad's presence would make forgiveness easy, but his presence was irrelevant. What was relevant was my hatred. It had substance and it had weight. So, with his wallet in my hand, I forgave my dad. I truly meant it. A half-century-old burden was actually lifted. If my dad should knock on my front door today, I would welcome him in, stand before him and say, "I forgive you," just as Christ asked his Father to forgive those who were putting him to death on the cross.

For something that happened so long ago, this was a very meaningful freedom. I returned my dad's wallet to the back of the drawer, and it felt like I was returning it to him — but not before I pocketed the three bucks.

CHAPTER 33

The Dance

When I released my anger and hatred toward my dad, I discovered I held a rare fond memory of him taking the family out on the Boston Whaler that became such a big part of my life.

My father purchased the boat in 1970 at the local water port in town. I was 7 years old.

I recall a day when Dad had honored Dolores, being the oldest sibling, by giving her the helm. With her small body barely tall enough to see through the window screen on top of the center console, she used her weight on the steering wheel to try to change course while Dad extended his arm, pointed in a northerly direction and said, "That way!" Try as she might, Dolores just couldn't straighten out the steering wheel. We rode around and around in circles and laughed.

Dad used the Boston Whaler for one summer and passed away the following winter, in January 1971. For whatever reason, Ma kept the boat, even though it sat dry dock at the local water port because we three kids were too young to take it out on our own and my mother was not comfortable taking us out on the open lake.

That all changed when my stepfather came along. You guessed it: He taught us the general upkeep and maintenance of the Boston Whaler and the proper handling and responsibilities when driving the boat. He also taught us how to waterski, how to pull skiers and how to dock the boat.

Every spring before taking out the boat, we had to prepare it for summer use. We sanded the wooden console and seats and applied two or more coats of varnish. We also were required to apply a coat of antifouling paint on the bottom hull, which we did while it was dry docked in the back yard. The Boston Whaler was used frequently during summers and created memories with family and friends that will last a lifetime — like chasing a zeppelin.

As my buddy and I were cruising a few miles off the coast of Lake Erie one day, we were directly beneath the enormous, dark shadow of an airship.

While the boat engine was at maximum speed, I stood behind the center console with the steering wheel in hand. I tilted my head back and stared straight up in awe at the size, the speed and the engine noise of the huge Goodyear blimp hovering no more than 50 feet above us, or so it seemed.

I craned my head toward the bow of the boat and noticed my buddy was hanging over the bow rails, standing on the tips of his toes with arms outstretched and hands unfolded like a child reaching for candy on a countertop. He was at the ready to grab hold of the blimp's trailing tie-down rope, which was dragging in the water a few feet away. We were gaining speed and closing in on it.

"What are you going to do with that rope?" I yelled. "I don't know!" he said.

"Wow! This is crazy! We have no plan!" I thought to myself. "How exciting is this?"

I held my breath as I watched my buddy's hand reach for the rope and realized he was within inches of it! Suddenly, the pilot raised the blimp, lifting its rope just out of reach. Then the pilot lowered the blimp again, and we realized he'd caught on to our game. But that didn't deter us as we continued to chase the rope for several more minutes, hoping the pilot would make a mistake. He didn't. We never did catch that rope. The blimp was simply too fast.

I had no idea what my buddy would have done if he had actually latched onto the trailing rope — other than fly airborne while dangling below the giant balloon — but we still laugh out loud when we reflect on it today.

A lot of our other adventures on the Boston Whaler revolved around water skiing with family and friends.

There was a summer day on the lake as high school kids when my friends and I kept pushing each other to try new ski tricks.

"If you don't fall you don't learn," I used to say to motivate us.

When my turn came around, I wanted to outdo all my friends. While water skiing backward on trick skis, I lowered my swim trunks and showed my friends the moon. I thought this was pretty funny and didn't realize my timing couldn't have been worse. Our boat was traveling right through a pack of fishing boats. The joke was on me. I came to a complete stop and slowly sank down into the water.

I turned around and could see my buddies roaring with laughter. They had pulled the throttle into neutral right in the middle of the pack of boats. As I sank further in the water, I looked at the crowd of angry fishermen giving me the death stare like I was a bucket of chum in shark-infested water. Not much more can be said about that, except it was still fun, even if it was at my own expense.

Then there was the day we had some fun at Ma's expense. Dolores, Paul and I somehow talked our mother into taking a turn water skiing. Why she trusted us, I'll never know. She jumped in the water and slipped a pair of wooden, Cypress Garden water skis on her feet for the first time. She was almost ready and was hanging on tightly to the ski rope when an expression crossed her face that told us she was having second thoughts. That expression was quickly replaced with fear when we yelled, "Hold onto the rope Ma! Here we go!"

We gunned the engine to maximum speed, which shot Ma's body out of the water like a clay pigeon. She held onto the ski rope for dear life and her face held a never-before-seen expression of absolute horror that made us roar with laughter. She yelled something that sounded somewhat like "SLOW DOWN!" We didn't. Ma held on and continued to ski as we continued to laugh until her body began to give out.

She let go of the ski rope, and her limp body hit the water and skipped across the surface like a flat rock. She was so exhausted we had to help hoist her listless body into the boat like a bag of wet sand. She landed inside the boat with a cathump. We asked her if she was all right, but she didn't respond. She was literally speechless.

"You did great out there Ma!" one of us said as she lay shaking. It must have taken her two months to recover from the muscle soreness that followed. Though Momma was always a trooper, I don't recall her ever water skiing again.

The Boston Whaler rested unused again for several years after my sister, brother and I had all grown and moved on to find jobs after college. Then, a few years after my stepfather passed in 2001, Ma asked if I'd like to take ownership of the boat, with the condition that I not sell it. I agreed and said it would be an honor.

Unfortunately, we had no way to transport it. We never had a need to until now. My stepfather had built and installed a hoist in the back yard that allowed us to lower the boat into the water and lift it up to a cradle when not in use. So Ma found an ad in the local paper for a boat trailer for sale, and she and a neighbor drove to the home to take a look.

The owner had an old wooden Lyman boat sitting on his trailer and a great deal of other items around his property. It looked like he was selling everything he owned. Ma negotiated a price for just the trailer, and the man dragged his Lyman off it. Then he lit the boat on fire and watched it burn. Apparently the guy was going through a bitter divorce. If she had known he was going to do that, Ma would have made an offer for the Lyman, as well.

A neighbor helped Ma hoist the Whaler onto the newly purchased trailer, and they drove it south and delivered it to me at my home in Alpharetta, Georgia.

I was already well into the final phase of vision loss and living in near blindness when I stood in my garage taking in the old Boston Whaler and rubbing my hands across her as if she were an old dog. Even with my poor eyesight, I could tell she didn't look good. After all those years of use followed by many years of sitting in dry dock, I could feel her weather-beaten body was in poor shape. The hull, console, seats, throttle and rub-rails were showing the Whaler's old age. The now-unusable corroded cables and the cracked wiring had left rust marks on the floor. The antifouling paint on the exterior of the hull was cracked and blistered, and there were a few puncture wounds in the fiberglass. I began to soak it all in and was faced with the overwhelming question of what to do with this thing. The work required was well beyond general upkeep. This was a major restoration project beyond my know-how, even with good vision. Now I was nearly blind. I walked away discouraged, but not entirely defeated. I needed some time to think about it.

Several months later, I walked through the garage on my way to put away the electric sander. I came to a stop in front of the boat. The Boston Whaler quietly grabbed my attention, and I stared at her for a few minutes. I unpacked the sander from its casing and plugged it in, then jumped into the boat. I started sanding a small area on the console just to see what would happen. This was the first step toward committing to this renovation project. I became motivated and determined to bring the boat back to life before I lost the remainder of my vision. I was hooked. My hopes and expectations were to complete this project and pass on the Whaler to my daughters someday. I wanted them to experience the joy this boat brought to me.

I broke the huge undertaking into several small projects. I began by sanding the wooden console and seats to bare-naked wood, which involved removing several coats of paint and varnish I applied when I was a kid. To restore the original beauty of the Philippine mahogany wood, I applied teak and a dozen coats of varnish. I searched the internet for ways to remove the rust marks and antifouling paint. I restored the entire interior and exterior hull so it looked like new. I had the cables, wiring and engine replaced. But I kept all the original pieces and parts I believed I could restore to maintain her original design and beauty.

It was a labor of love and took years to complete. By the time I was done and put her back in the water, it had been more than 25 years since the summer of 1987, when I last stood behind the center console on Lake Erie. I placed a hand on the throttle and the other hand on the ignition key switch, and it felt like I was slipping on a pair of customized gloves. I turned the key, and immediately her body came to life. I felt like Dr. Frankenstein should be beside me exclaiming, "She's alive!" My hand naturally moved from the key to the steering wheel as I pulled the throttle into reverse. The trailer slowly loosened its grip on the boat, releasing the Boston Whaler back into the water where she belonged. I was astonished and thrilled beyond words. She looked and felt so good. Better than ever, I thought.

I was so grateful God gave me the ability, with my limited vision, to complete this project that was so important to me. I was ready to create more memories with my family and friends.

Like my stepfather had done with me, I taught my wife and my daughters all about the proper handling and responsibilities that came with driving the boat, how to waterski, how to pull a skier and to dock the boat.

On her 50th Birthday, I entered my 1969 Boston Whaler in the Antique Classic Boat Show in a small, Georgia town on Hartwell Lake, just across the border from Anderson, South Carolina, where my wife and I live today. I entered her to honor my father, my stepfather and my mother. It was my way of thanking them for all the great memories we had and to thank Ma for keeping the boat so new memories could be created now and for years to come.

I don't drive the Whaler anymore, but this old man can still waterski now that my wife and daughters can pull me. Waterskiing nearly blind is a whole new experience, but it still produces the same thrill of freedom it always has. When we're exhausted from skiing, we'll turn off the engine, jump in the water with a float and spend quality time together talking, laughing and relaxing.

That Boston Whaler has turned out to be an amazing conduit for conversations, laughter, friendships and memories. It has been a focal point that has touched the lives of four generations of our family and countless friends.

In 2018, the year Ma passed away, we held a small reunion with my siblings at my home. Our dock served as our gathering place, and the old Boston Whaler was tied there. It was the first time in many years my sister and brother had seen her. After a while, Dolores, her husband and I stepped onboard the boat and headed out toward the open lake. I gave Dolores the helm. She began to dust off the memories and was soon joyously reliving the old days. As she was driving, I stood to my feet, extended an arm, pointed in a northerly direction and said "That way!" She let out a quick laugh but caught herself. She was silent for a moment, then a tear rolled down her cheek. She remembered.

As the reunion came to a close, I stood alone on the dock listening to the calm waters that cradled the boat and gently rocked her back and forth. Together they played the distinctive and familiar song that mesmerizes the mind and soothes the soul. All I had to do was put my hands on the boat for years of memories to come flooding back. Like the memory of that day long ago on Lake Erie when I cut the motor and laid down. The freeze-frame portrait of the sunset that evening was still clear in my mind. I remembered the anger I felt toward God and wondering what the future would hold for me.

As I recalled all this, I shook my head at how silly I had been to question that God knew my future and would use it for good. I thank him for my remarkable journey. If I had known how my future would unfold at the time, I may have chosen to avoid the hard road and the pain that lay ahead. I would have missed the most important part — the joy of knowing Christ and walking through my challenges and struggles with him leading me. I would have missed drawing from the well and drinking from the water of salvation (Isaiah 12:2-3).

Garth Brooks precisely captures my sentiments in the lyrics of his hit song "The Dance".

> "And now I'm glad I didn't know
> The way it all would end, the way it all would go
> Our lives are better left to chance
> I could have missed the pain
> But I'd have had to miss the dance"

Well said and so true. I could have missed the pain, but there was no way I'd have missed the dance.

The Queen

S omeone once asked if I had a bucket
list of activities I hope to complete before I totally lose
my vision. I could honestly and without hesitation reply, "No."

I don't have a personal bucket list because I try to live
it out every day. My bucket list lifestyle began when I professed Christ as my savior and gave my life to him. That was
when I truly began to live each moment with passion, and I
will continue to do so until the last activity on Jesus's list for
me is fulfilled, which will be the day I'm called to rest in the
shadow of the Almighty.

Texas Governor Greg Abbott used to have the ability
to walk. Today, he's paralyzed and uses a wheelchair. Gov.
Abbott provided a sense of the bucket list life I'm talking
about when he responded to those who questioned God by
reflecting on his own experiences. "I've done more AFTER
the accident that left me paralyzed than before that accident. With God all things are possible," he said. "God didn't
cause the accident that left me paralyzed, but he did help
me persevere over that enormous challenge." His comments
are so true.

Something happens to a person when they suddenly find themselves in the middle of a storm, looking up from beneath the massive waves that cover them and wondering how on earth they are going to make it through.

As you now know, I've made multiple attempts to sail through the hurricane on my own without Christ as my centerboard. It left my sailboat completely exposed, vulnerable and unstable, and I capsized repeatedly. It was an experience beyond failure and frustration that left me totally exhausted. It was a feeling of absolute hopelessness.

I once thought it was impossible, but I have learned how to truly live through Christ. He showed me the passageway that sheltered my boat from the winds and carried me into calmer waters. Like Gov. Abbott, God gave me the perseverance to get through some enormous challenges. Since I accepted Christ, I've done more during the days of losing my vision than I ever dreamed possible.

If I could illustrate my point using a line graph, it would show joy, love, patience, kindness, gentleness, self-discipline, courage, fearlessness, selflessness, passion, strength and hope all increasing with a steep incline. I know this phenomenon seems strange while someone is going blind, yet I would draw a second graph that further defies logic. While the first graph is shooting upward, the second is simultaneously showing bitterness, resentment, fear, shame, selfishness, anxiety and stress all decreasing with a steep decline.

I can tell you with certainty, before I surrendered my life to Christ the lines on these graphs were the opposite. My suffering had brought out the worst of me. The level of hope in my heart was squashed by the weight of fear. Having Christ in my life has turned the tables. Now, the hope in my heart far outweighs any negative feelings, including the fear of my circumstances. Christ has brought out the best of me.

How can this possibly be?

The best way I can describe it is to compare it to a game of chess. The queen is the most powerful and dominant piece on the chessboard. She's the only one who can move in all directions — forward, backward, side-to-side and diagonally. Generally speaking, if you lose your queen, you're in trouble and, most likely, will soon lose the game.

In the game of life, my vision was my queen. I lost her and, though I struggled mightily to play the game, I nearly lost my life because I didn't know how to survive without this piece I so heavily relied on. But on my way toward defeat, the queen was replaced with hope. Having hope and faith on the game board, I became a much better, much stronger, much more determined player without the queen than I was when I still held her advantage. This is the hope Christ provides. It is not a short-lived "shazam" moment. Hope is sustainable and constant, regardless of the circumstances.

I still have my ups and downs. I still suffer like everybody else. But I know I will persevere through those challenges because with Christ I'm a much better player.

CHAPTER 35

The Strong Finish

Throughout this book, I've openly documented my experiences and how my faith developed on my journey. Answering God's call from that off-script message definitely made my journey much more interesting. I asked Christ to come along with me for the ride ... or, more accurately, he asked me to come along and let him drive.

As I said earlier, fullbacks don't often get the call to run the ball, but the moment God called my number was the most significant in my life. I had to decide — accept his call, wrap both my arms around my soul and run toward daylight, or let the ball drop and continue living in my own strength, trapped in the storm.

Regardless of how small or how tempestuous our storms, it is not humanly possible to escape them. We all suffer at some level at some point in our lives. We can't avoid or ignore it.

In the midst of our deepest storms, I believe it also is not humanly possible to deny God's call to decide if we will follow him. I believe each of us will eventually reach that moment when putting off the decision for later has suddenly accelerated to now. What will you choose? Accept Christ, or reject him and continue down your own path?

When God calls you, don't be afraid of disappointments like I was. Don't be afraid of being laughed at or ridiculed by naysayers. Look at it from this viewpoint: a thorny crown was forced into Jesus Christ's head and spikes were driven through his hands and feet. He was the lamb who was slain to give us life, yet he asked God his father to forgive the naysayers.

Forgive your naysayers and move on with determination and purpose. It may sound unthinkable and unimaginable, but I encourage you to think it and imagine it — then do it: Follow God when he calls you. Accept his gift. Then look up Romans 5:3-5 in the Bible and read it out loud.

"Not only so, but we also glory in our sufferings, because we know that suffering produces perseverance; perseverance, character; and character, hope. And hope does not put us to shame, because God's love has been poured out into our hearts through the Holy Spirit, who has been given to us."

Read it again and try to memorize it. The verse is difficult, but it is the simple truth. It is just one of many that provides an answer to our deepest needs during rough waters and storms.

I encourage you to pray for Christ to come into your life, to be your centerboard, to right your capsized sailboat and provide stability through your storms. I encourage you to pray to keep your keel — your soul — centered on Christ. I encourage you to pray for the courage to move. I encourage you to pray to shed the weight of your frustration and fears.

Fuzz and I would be honored to lead the way, to take out that blitzing linebacker so you can sprint toward daylight and find your path toward Christ.

The final score in this game is irrelevant. What's relevant in the game of life is who's standing beneath the old scoreboard to receive us with open arms: Jesus Christ.

Profession of Faith

This is the full story of my faith journey that was shared with my church.

I never anticipated I would have a story to share. I never anticipated so much in my life.

I would never have guessed I would graduate from college when doctors had told my parents my severe hearing loss wouldn't allow me to make it beyond elementary school.

I certainly wouldn't have guessed in my 20s I'd learn I had an incurable disease that would rob me of my vision as I aged.

Knowing I would someday go blind, I never anticipated I would be able to work at awesome companies over many years and be entrusted with awesome global responsibilities.

I couldn't have fathomed my wife wouldn't let my disease stop her from saying yes when I proposed or that she would keep her vows and stick with me through so many trials. I never anticipated being married to her would bring such awesome joy as we grow in Christ together and grow old together.

I never anticipated the joy of raising daughters, how the knowledge that one day I wouldn't be able to see their faces would spur me to work hard at being a great dad and how proud I would be of the women they've become.

And I couldn't have imagined the awesome mentors placed in my life who would leave a very positive impression on me, that would teach me hard work and that life was not meant to be fair on my terms.

But I also didn't anticipate, as I tried to control my disease on my own, I would fail miserably. I never thought one day I would drop to my knees from the sheer weight of frustration, embarrassment, fear, anger, anxiety, worries, bitterness, resentment toward others, isolation and doubts.

I never anticipated one Sunday morning I would feel like I was the sole recipient of our pastor's message from God that would forever change the course of my life.

I had no idea the Holy Spirit could and would draw me close to Christ and strengthen my faith even while I was losing my vision.

I most assuredly never thought, after suffering severe physical and emotional falls over the years, I would change from demanding to know when enough is enough to praying for the courage to stand on my feet and move without fear. I never anticipated God would hear my prayers and strangers would ask if they could pray for me.

I never anticipated the day would come when I would once again be able to walk across a street on my own with a white cane, that I could overcome the countless number of naysayers over the years who asserted: "You can't do it." "You won't ever." "You never will." Through Christ, I could and I did, and it taught me to never underestimate the power of faith in Christ.

> "Surely God is my salvation; I will trust and not be afraid. The Lord, the Lord himself, is my strength and my defense; He has become my salvation. With joy you will draw water from the wells of salvation." – Isaiah 12:2-3

To say the process of losing my vision and hearing was difficult and humbling is an understatement, not only for me but for my family, as well. This verse is one where the rubber meets the road for me and is undeniably difficult to fulfill. I am trying to comprehend this verse to the fullest every day. I may never master it, but I will never give up trying. I want to honor God the best I know how by letting him know I am forever grateful and I will follow.

You now know the truth. If there's one person listening and paying attention when you're struggling with something, it's God. Shed the weight of frustration and fear. I encourage you to pray for courage to stand on your feet and move, and don't be afraid.

Why I Decided to
Write This Book

"**N**o. That's not going to happen."
That was my response several years ago when I first was approached about writing my story. There's not much of a story to tell, I thought. I also objected to sharing my private business with others.

"Everybody has their own sufferings," I said. "They just keep it to themselves."

Yet people continued to encourage me to tell my story — and I continued to resist. I was not seeing what others were seeing in my life, and I truly didn't believe there was much to tell. Then, one day, someone struck a nerve.

An acquaintance of mine said to me very intently, "There are people hurting out there, Mike." That got my undivided attention.

"There are people, young and old, who are losing their eyesight right now, and they're scared and have no idea how to handle this," he continued. "There are soldiers who are coming home struggling with permanent injuries. There are couples struggling to figure out how to support one another during times of suffering. There are children in wheelchairs, people struggling with AIDS, people struggling with addiction and parents with young disabled children who all could use some encouragement."

I heard him loud and clear, and I could not deny his words. I knew he spoke the truth. I could relate to all those people he mentioned because I had been there and had hurt deeply. Yet I kept my story under wraps because I had no idea how I could possibly reach out or try to help others change their perspective on the future.

A recollection surfaced of some blog messages I read online several years before. One was written by the mother of a disabled child and another was written by a young lady. The mother's blog had been written in pure panic right after her child was diagnosed with Retinitis Pigmentosa. She was desperately seeking, from a parent's perspective, direction and advice about what to do for her child and how to handle this situation. She was lost.

The young lady who wrote the other message was struggling to live her everyday life while dealing with Usher Syndrome. She was on the edge of taking her own life. The last sentence she typed read, "I can no longer take this." She then went dark without ever responding to the person with whom she had been communicating.

I have no idea what happened to this young lady or to this mother, but I've never forgotten about them.

The conversation with my acquaintance was still nagging me in late 2018, when I finally said "Okay," then walked to my home office and powered up the computer. I reviewed my profession of faith and decided to use it as a framework for my book, expanding on it with greater detail. The focus was to share my life's journey and experiences: Who I thought I was and my lack of faith in God as I faced my disease. Finding and strengthening my faith in God and discovering the person God knew I was as I faced the future he had planned for me. Usher Syndrome Type II's negative impact on my hearing and vision. Depression and anger, but also humor and joy. The importance of family, good friends and very strong mentors.

I began to type, but became discouraged as I spent most of my time searching for my cursor as I moved my mouse. I made very slow progress. I was aware there were applications available to assist the visually impaired when using the computer, but they didn't seem worth the time it would take to learn how to use them.

Then, while training with Fuzz at Leader Dogs for the Blind in April 2019, I received another motivating kick in the pants. A guy with the organization encouraged me to get my story out. He said the exact same thing that had caught my attention before: "People are hurting out there, Mike."

In search of a better method to write quickly, I tried composing an email on my iPhone and found it to be an effective way to type out my story. The length of the story taking shape eventually forced me to create two separate emails with subject lines of Part 1 and Part 2, and I saved them as drafts to remain in edit mode. My wife then helped me retrieve the emails and put them into a Word document. The whole process was a bit convoluted and time consuming, but it was a process that worked for me and my vision capabilities at the time.

While writing my story, I'd be sitting quietly indoors or on my daily runs when thoughts, old memories and analogies came flooding into my mind, and I tried my best to pour them out and capture them in detail in my email book drafts. I used them to describe circumstances, events or experiences in ways I hope someone might be able to relate to. Some analogies were used as a tribute to those who had an impact on my life or in memory of those who have passed away.

Their teachings and my experiences with them made a lasting impression on me, and they live on in my thoughts and in my writing.

My hopes and prayers are that the words in this book will reach out to those who need to hear the message that has been written through the story of my life; that it would reach that mother and her disabled child, and they would hear words of encouragement; that the message of hope would find that young lady suffering somewhere out there and she, and those like her, would find motivation and inspiration and inspire others as a result; that the message will reach out to as many people as possible who are suffering from illnesses and physical challenges. If that is you, I pray my story uplifts you and gives you hope and strength as you consider how you will live out your life's journey when faced with struggles and suffering.

Tributes and Memories

I thank the many people who encouraged me to write my story and share my faith. I'm not sure if it was what you had envisioned. There was so much more to it than what may have appeared on the surface. People often see me holding my white cane or with Fuzz by my side and a smile on my face. They do not know how much I've been through to be able to wear that smile. Even many of those who encouraged me did not know the depth or details involved in my journey. I have attempted to tell my story with transparency. To tell it in any other way would be to omit the truth. I believe God is the author of life, and he called me to share the story of my life with others. I thank him for placing all you encouragers in my life to push me until I did it.

To my spiritual mentors:

Thank you to Pastor Crawford Loritts, whom God used to speak the off-script message while I sat in the sanctuary at Fellowship Bible Church in Roswell, Georgia.

Thank you to Fellowship Bible Church Men's Bible Study Group and Fellowship Institute Roswell, Georgia.

Thank you to the NewSpring Men's Mentoring Bible Study Group in Anderson, South Carolina.

In memory:

A "fine red wine sky" is a tribute to my mother and her closest friends, who often shared a glass of red wine and a lot of laughs.

The story of the Regatta sailboat race is in memory of a childhood buddy and classmate, Ed Babson. My memories of fun and laughter with him still live on.

"Big right tackle" is in memory of classmate and teammate Terry Holman, who actually was our big right tackle. A people mover on the field and a gentle giant off the field.

"Fidgety fingers" is in memory of classmate and teammate Paul Lewis. I recall the guys joking about Paul's never-resting fidgety fingers that constantly pressed the car radio buttons far before the song was even close to ending. When not pressing buttons, his fidgety fingers could be found playing an imaginary keyboard on the dashboard.

Other tributes:

A tribute to the skydive adventure my wife and daughters gave me for my 50th birthday.

There's nothing like the feeling of freefalling at over 100 miles per hour at 15,000 feet for several minutes before parachuting back to earth.

Credits and Resources

Books:

Stanley, Andy. *Louder than Words*. (United States: Multnomah Books, 2004), Chapter 2, Kindle.

Buford, Bob. *Half Time: Changing Your Game Plan from Success to Significance*. (United States: Zondervan Publishing Company, 2004)

Scripture quotations taken from The Holy Bible, New International Version® NIV® Copyright © 1973, 1978, 1984, 2011 by Biblica, Inc.™ Used by permission. All rights reserved worldwide.

Organizations:

Leader Dogs for the Blind: https://www.leaderdog.org/

Foundation Fighting Blindness:
https://www.fightingblindness.org/

NORD (National Organization for Rare Disorders): https://rarediseases.org/for-patients-and-families/information-resources/rare-disease-information/

Mike Garrigan, age 5.

My father and mother.

My mother and step-father on Parent Night (junior year of highschool).

Mike (number 30) carrying the ball. I had no idea that the outer band of the storm had already reached the ball carrier. In contrast to this picture, I would later learn to utilize a white cane and a guide dog to avoid running into people.

Becky and Mike on their wedding day in 1994.

Becky and the girls (3 and 7 years old) on Halloween.

Daddy's girls.

The girls at a bridal shower (all grown up).

Mike running in his yellow blind runner's vest (the giant bumble bee).

Coach Mentis and Mike pictured at the football reunion.

Mike pictured with his white cane that he received at Leader Dogs for The Blind.

Mike waterskiing on Lake Hartwell (2020). Like riding a bike with eyes closed you never forget how to waterski. As an old blind man today the experience is still exhilarating.

The 1969 Boston Whaler restored. Such a special boat for the lives that she touched and great memories that remain. New adventures and memory making await.

Bashful boy, Fuzz.

Fuzz in the harness leading Mike.